PREVENTING JOB BURNOUT
Transforming Work Pressures Into Productivity

Revised Edition

Beverly A. Potter, Ph.D

A FIFTY-MINUTE™ SERIES BOOK

CRISP PUBLICATIONS, INC.
Menlo Park, California

PREVENTING JOB BURNOUT
Transforming Work Pressures Into Productivity
Revised Edition

Beverly A. Potter, Ph.D.

CREDITS
Managing Editor: **Kathleen Barcos**
Editor: **Janis Paris**
Typesetting: **ExecuStaff**
Cover Design: **Carol Harris**
Artwork: **Phil Frank, Creative Media Services**

Printed in the United States of America by Bawden Printing Company.

Distribution to the U.S. Trade:

National Book Network, Inc.
4720 Boston Way
Lanham, MD 20706
1-800-462-6420

Library of Congress Catalog Card Number 95-78810
Potter, Beverly A.
Preventing Job Burnout
ISBN 1-56052-357-3

This book is printed on recyclable paper with soy ink.

PREFACE

If you've ever had a bad day at work—and who hasn't—then you have an idea of how immobilizing burnout can be. If having a bad day at work has become the standard rather than the exception, then it is likely that you are a victim of job burnout. But work doesn't have to be a chore. There are specific actions you can take, starting today, to beat job burnout and transform work pressure into productivity. Introducing you to these techniques and showing you how to use them is the purpose of this book.

Preventing Job Burnout is a practical guide. You will learn what job burnout is, what causes it, and how to assess the burnout potential of your job. And you will learn how to identify what is eroding your motivation and enthusiasm for your job. More importantly, you will learn eight strategies for beating job burnout and preventing it in the future.

Preventing Job Burnout is a fun book. As you complete the exercises and carry out the suggested activities you will learn more about yourself, particularly how you function—on and off—the job. Learning about yourself can be fun, and knowing yourself better increases your ability to control your job and your life. When you feel you can control what happens to you, your health tends to improve, your relationships tend to get better, and you tend to perform better.

Preventing Job Burnout is not a book to be read one time from cover to cover. It is a book to return to again and again for refueling and new ideas about how to handle difficult situations on the job. Enjoy.

ABOUT THIS BOOK

Preventing Job Burnout is not like most books. It has a unique "self-paced" format that encourages a reader to become personally involved. Designed to be "read with a pencil," there is an abundance of exercises, activities, assessments, and cases that invite participation.

This book is an action-packed resource designed to help readers who may be struggling with feelings of job burnout. Following the eight paths to personal power, the reader will learn to transform work pressures into productivity, which will lead to greater happiness and more on-the-job satisfaction.

Preventing Job Burnout can be used effectively in a number of ways. Here are some possibilities:

▶ **Individual Study.** Because the book is self-instructional, all that is needed is a quiet place, some time, and a pencil. By completing the activities and exercises, a reader should not only receive valuable feedback, but also practical ideas for improving the quality of your work life.

▶ **Workshops and Seminars.** This book is ideal for reading prior to a workshop or seminar. With the basics in hand, the quality of participation will improve. More time can be spent on concept extensions and applications during the program. The book is also effective when a trainer distributes it at the beginning of a session and leads participants through the contents.

▶ **Informal Study Groups.** Thanks to the format, brevity and low cost, this book is ideal for "brown-bag" or other informal group sessions.

There are other possibilities that depend on the objectives, program, or ideas of the user. One thing is certain; even after it has been read, this book will serve as excellent reference material that can be easily reviewed.

ABOUT THE AUTHOR

Beverly A. Potter, Ph.D., earned her doctorate in counseling psychology from Stanford University and her masters in vocational rehabilitation from San Francisco State University. She has provided management and self-development training for over 20 years.

Beverly combines western behavior change psychology with eastern metaphysical principles to present a dynamic, practical and inspirational approach to career issues. She has worked with a wide range of corporations, governmental agencies, associations and colleges providing training seminars and motivational keynote speeches. She welcomes feedback and questions. She can be reached at P.O. Box 1035, Berkeley, California, 94701.

Other books by Beverly Potter include

Beating Job Burnout: How to Transform Work Pressure into Productivity; Finding a Path with a Heart: How to Go from Burnout to Bliss; The Way of the Ronin: Riding the Waves of Change at Work; Turning Around: Keys to Motivation and Productivity; Brain Boosters: Foods and Drugs that Make You Smarter; and *Drug Testing at Work: A Guide for Employers and Employees.*

CONTENTS

WHAT IS JOB BURNOUT?

Without work, all life goes rotten, but when work is soulless, life stifles and dies.

—Albert Camus

Job burnout is an impairment of motivation to work, resulting in a growing inability to mobilize interest and abilities. More and more common in today's complex world, burnout begins with small warning signals.

Burnout Warning Signals:

Feelings of frustration

Emotional outbursts

"Why bother?" attitude

Sense of alienation

Substandard performance

Increased use of drugs and alcohol

If unheeded, these symptoms can progress until a person dreads going to work. Even worse, burnout tends to spread to all aspects of a person's life. Rarely is a person burned out at work, yet energized and enthusiastic at home.

This is the beginning of the downward spiral of job burnout.

BURNOUT SYMPTOMS

Following are the common symptoms of job burnout:

NEGATIVE EMOTIONS: Occasional feelings of frustration, anger, depression, dissatisfaction and anxiety are normal parts of living and working. But people caught in the burnout cycle usually experience these negative emotions more and more often until they become chronic. Eventually, the person complains of emotional fatigue.

INTERPERSONAL PROBLEMS: Feeling emotionally drained makes interacting with people on the job and at home more difficult. When inevitable conflicts arise, the burnout victim is likely to overreact with an emotional outburst or intense hostility. This makes communication with co-workers, friends and family increasingly difficult. The victim also tends to withdraw from social interactions. The tendency to withdraw is most pronounced among helping professionals who often become aloof and inaccessible to the very people they are expected to help.

HEALTH PROBLEMS: As the person's emotional reserves are depleted and the quality of relationships deteriorates, the burnout victim's physical resilience declines. Minor ailments, such as colds, headaches, insomnia and backaches become more frequent. There is a general feeling of being tired and rundown.

DECLINING PERFORMANCE: During the burnout process a person may become bored and unable to get excited about projects. In other cases, the burnout victim may discover that concentrating on projects is increasingly difficult. Efficiency suffers and quality of output declines.

SUBSTANCE ABUSE: To cope with the stress associated with job conflict and declining performance, the person will often consume more alcohol, eat more or eat less, use more drugs (including prescription and over-the-counter remedies), smoke more cigarettes, eat more sweets and drink more coffee. This increased substance abuse further compounds problems.

FEELINGS OF MEANINGLESSNESS: Feelings of "so what" and "why bother" become more and more predominant. This is particularly common among burnout victims who were once very enthusiastic and dedicated. Enthusiasm is replaced by cynicism. Working seems pointless.

WHO'S SUSCEPTIBLE TO BURNOUT?

Helping professionals, such as social workers, nurses, teachers and police officers, are the hardest hit by burnout. Often they become cynical and negative, and sometimes overtly hostile towards their clients. Other burnout-prone professions include: those that require exacting attention, such as air traffic controllers; those that deal with life or death decisions, such as heart surgeons; those that require working under demanding time schedules, such as television news crews; or those that involve detailed work, such as bookkeeping; those that are socially criticized, such as nuclear plant supervisors; and many others. The fact is, *any* person, in any profession, at any level can become a candidate for burnout. No one is immune.

Are You At Risk of Burning Out?

No One Is Immune!

TEST: Are You Burning Out?

Review your life over the last six months, both at work and away from work. Then read each of the following items and rate how often the symptom is true of you.

> *Rating scale:*
> Rarely true   1   2   3   4   5   Usually true

_____   **1.** I feel tired even though I've gotten adequate sleep.

_____   **2.** I am dissatisfied with my work.

_____   **3.** I feel sad for no apparent reason.

_____   **4.** I am forgetful.

_____   **5.** I am irritable and snap at people.

_____   **6.** I avoid people at work and in my private life.

_____   **7.** I have trouble sleeping because of worrying about work.

_____   **8.** I get sick a lot more than I used to.

_____   **9.** My attitude about work is "why bother?"

_____   **10.** I get into conflicts at work.

_____   **11.** My job performance is not up to par.

_____   **12.** I use alcohol and/or drugs to feel better.

_____   **13.** Communicating with people is a strain.

_____   **14.** I can't concentrate on my work like I once could.

_____   **15.** I am bored with my work.

_____   **16.** I work hard but accomplish little.

_____ **17.** I feel frustrated with my work.

_____ **18.** I don't like going to work.

_____ **19.** Social activities are draining.

_____ **20.** Sex is not worth the effort.

_____ **21.** I watch television most of the time when not working.

_____ **22.** I don't have much to look forward to in my work.

_____ **23.** I worry about work during off hours.

_____ **24.** My feelings about work interfere with my personal life.

_____ **25.** My work seems pointless.

_____ **Total**

Scoring: **25–50** You're doing well.
51–75 You're okay if you take preventative action.
76–100 You're a candidate for job burnout.
101–125 You're burning out.

This test is reprinted by permission from *Beating Job Burnout: How to Transform Work Pressure Into Productivity*, Dr. Beverly Potter, Ronin Publishing, © 1993: Beverly A. Potter.

MOTIVATIONAL NUTRIENTS

Nurture Motivation to Prevent Job Burnout.

Just as the body needs vitamins and proteins, certain "nutrients" are also essential to sustain high motivation. These include getting "wins" for good work and having feelings of control.

Burnout is neither a physical ailment nor a neurosis, even though it has both physical and psychological effects. It is an inability to get together enough interest to act. Motivation to perform is diminished or extinguished. To prevent job burnout, you need to maintain motivation.

"Wins" for Good Work

Motivation is determined largely by what happens *after* you act. You are unlikely to continue doing something that makes you lose or that brings you nothing. If your motivation is to remain high, you must get "wins" for performing. There are two kinds of wins: positive, where you win by gaining a positive, and negative, where you win by avoiding something negative.

Positive Wins

A *positive win* occurs when you *do something*

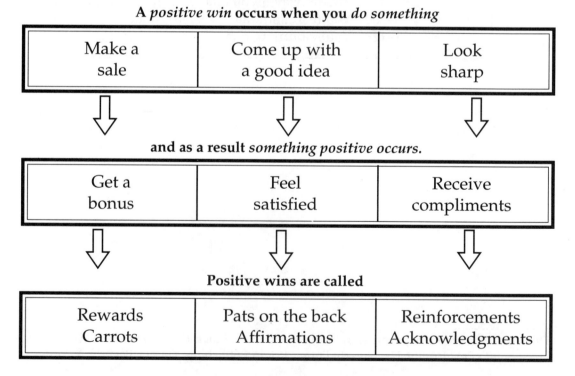

Make a sale	Come up with a good idea	Look sharp

and as a result *something positive occurs*.

Get a bonus	Feel satisfied	Receive compliments

Positive wins are called

Rewards Carrots	Pats on the back Affirmations	Reinforcements Acknowledgments

Negative Wins

A *negative win* occurs when a *negative situation exists*

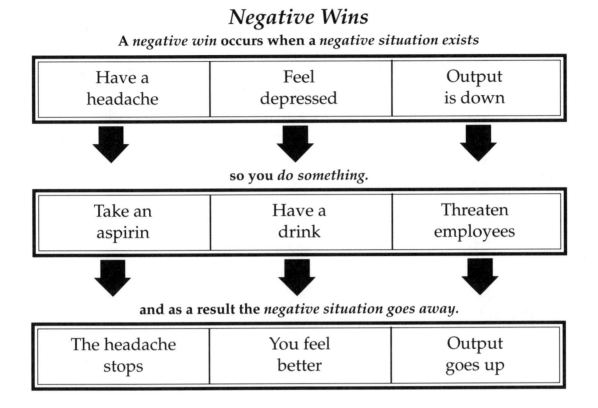

Have a headache	Feel depressed	Output is down

so you *do something*.

Take an aspirin	Have a drink	Threaten employees

and as a result the *negative situation goes away*.

The headache stops	You feel better	Output goes up

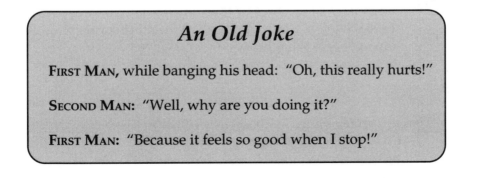

An Old Joke

FIRST MAN, while banging his head: "Oh, this really hurts!"

SECOND MAN: "Well, why are you doing it?"

FIRST MAN: "Because it feels so good when I stop!"

IDENTIFY THE WINS

What positive and negative wins can you find in each of the following cases? What do you predict will happen in the future?

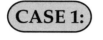 Sally worked all weekend putting the final touches on her presentation to the sales force. When she made the presentation, she had to pause several times for the laughter at her jokes to subside. When she finished, the sales reps gave her an enthusiastic standing ovation.

Sally's wins _____

In the future Sally will probably _____

_____

 Bill's boss hates idleness. If she thinks Bill doesn't have enough to do she quickly assigns him more work. Bill just noticed his boss patrolling the aisles so he quickly lowered his head and wrote meaningless notes on a pad. Bill's boss nodded approvingly as she walked by his desk.

Bill's wins _____

In the future Bill will probably _____

_____

 Supervisor Ralph has an open door policy, and Jim takes advantage of it. Three or four times a day Jim drops by Ralph's office to tell him the latest gossip from the sports page. Ralph always stops what he's doing and listens carefully.

Jim's wins _____

In the future Jim will probably _____

_____

CASE 4: Ralph was recently promoted to supervisor. To prepare for the job he took a training course where he learned about the importance of an "open door" policy. Ralph implemented it and people drop by several times a day, but they rarely talk about work. One employee, Jim, told him that he's a "great guy to work for." Because of the constant interruptions, Ralph can't get his work done and must take it home at night. His wife has begun complaining because they never go out any more.

Ralph's wins _____

In the future Ralph will probably _____

_____

CASE 5: Even though Helen has taken several management courses, she can't seem to break the procrastination habit. It was her responsibility to write a proposal for a million dollar grant. The fate of her department hung in the balance. As usual, Helen procrastinated. For two weeks she was paralyzed with guilt and fear. However, she finally got started and, with the help of some pills she gets from a friend, managed to work straight through two nights with only a couple of 15-minute naps. She miraculously got the proposal done just in time. Feeling enormously relieved, Helen went home and collapsed.

Helen's wins _____

In the future Helen will probably _____

_____

IDENTIFY THE WINS (continued)

 CASE 6: Willie's boss, Hank, is easily rattled. Willie delights in getting Hank to react and baits him at every opportunity. Hank is particularly irritated when Willie is late. He's talked to Willie a number of times about it but Willie continues his lateness. Willie returned 15 minutes late from a break today and Hank was furious. Trying to be calm, Hank blurted out, "You're late again!" The gum Hank was chewing flew out of his mouth and hit Willie on the cheek. Knowing that several other guys were watching, Willie retorted, "I'm going to have you arrested for assault with a deadly weapon." Everyone in the office broke into uncontrollable laughter as Hank stomped off. Several times in the following week the other guys retold the story and said, "Way to go, Willie!"

Willie's wins _____

In the future Willie will probably _____

_____

DO YOUR ANSWERS MATCH THE AUTHOR'S?
READ ON TO FIND OUT.

Case Study Discussions

CASE 1: Sally received two strong positive wins: the laughter and the standing ovation. Chances are she will continue putting extra time into her presentations and will tell a lot of jokes during the delivery.

CASE 2: By looking busy, Bill gets the negative win of avoiding additional work. Bill will probably work slower to stretch his assignments out and engage in meaningless activity in order to look busy whenever he sees his boss approaching his desk.

CASE 3: Ralph's attention to Jim's talking about sports is a positive win for Jim. A hidden win is that talking about sports is probably more enjoyable than working. It's no wonder he drops into Ralph's office several times a day. As long as Ralph continues to listen to Jim's stories he should expect Jim to talk about sports.

CASE 4: People dropping into Ralph's office and Jim's friendly comment are positive wins for Ralph. However, he's also receiving strong punishments. He cannot complete his work during the day so he has to work after hours at home, and his wife complains about it. Ralph is a good candidate for job burnout.

CASE 5: Helen's procrastination habit is supported by negative wins. Her procrastination creates tremendous anxiety. When she finally does write the proposal she wins by succeeding in avoiding disaster. Further, she experiences relief, which feels very good and is another win. The cycle is compounded by her drug use. Helen is a good candidate for job burnout.

CASE 6: Willie's lateness is supported by strong positive wins. Not only did he succeed in unnerving Hank and making him look foolish in front of everyone, he also received much admiration from the other guys. Willie will most likely continue being late.

12

FEELINGS OF CONTROL

Damned-if-you-do, damned-if-you-don't situations create feelings of helplessness and weaken motivation.

You've got to choose!

WORK AS HELL

In Greek mythology, Sisyphus, an evil king, was condemned to Hades to forever roll a big rock up a mountain, and then the rock always rolled back down again. This version of Hell is suffered every day by people with forever full in-baskets, or who work under unrelenting pressure, or who work with clients who don't get better.

Sustaining Motivation

To sustain motivation, you must see a relationship between what you do and what happens to you. In other words, you must feel you can influence what happens to you—either good or bad—*by what you do.*

Giving yourself pats on the back or self-acknowledgment is essential for developing "working for" motivation.

Pat Yourself on the Back

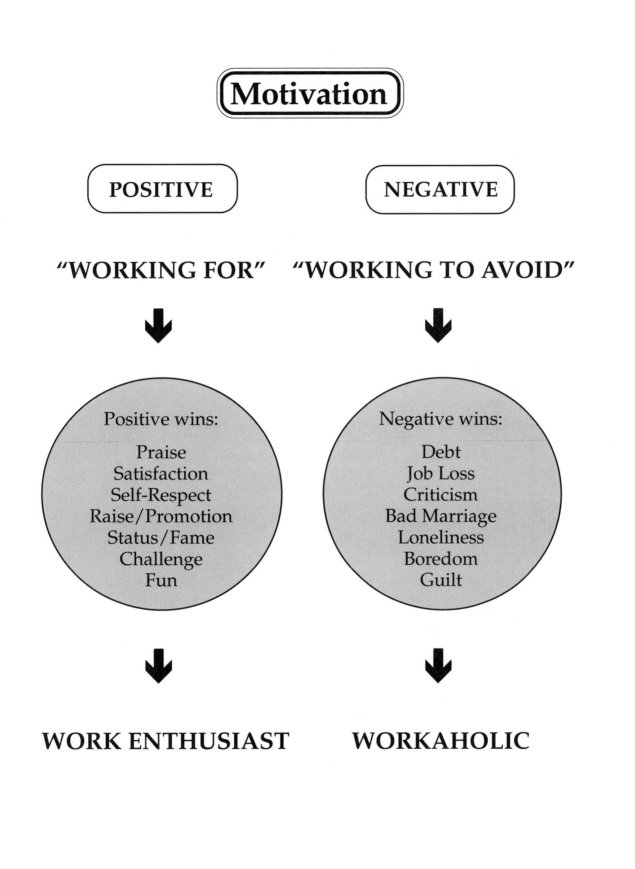

Learned Helplessness: A Scientific Study

Pairs of dogs, matched for a variety of characteristics, were placed one at a time in a room with a shock-grid floor. One dog from the pair could do something to turn off the shock; the other could do nothing.

When first shocked both dogs jumped, yelped and ran around frantically. In an effort to escape, the dog in the "controllable" situation knocked a lever, turning off the shock. This dog learned quickly. Every time the dog was put in the room, it quickly ran to the lever to turn off the shock. This dog was highly motivated by the negative win of avoiding the shock.

In the "uncontrollable" situation there was nothing the second dog could do to turn off the shock. Just like the first dog, it tried to figure out how to turn off the shock until the dog learned it was helpless. Then the dog gave up, lay down on the floor and took it. The dog no longer even tried to escape.

Later, the dog that had learned it was helpless was put into the room with the lever for turning off the shock. But the dog still just lay on the floor and took the shock. Even when the door was left wide open, the dog did not attempt to escape—it just lay there. Even though the situation had changed, the dog had *learned that it was helpless* and continued to act as if it were.

When the dog "learned" it was helpless first it stopped trying. Its motivation to escape was gone. The dog also displayed many negative emotions. It yelped and growled, then it whimpered and eventually just lay there. Something had halted the dog's ability to learn that things had changed and it could do something.

Powerlessness at work can affect you in the same way. Feelings of powerlessness cause burnout.

Uncontrollable work situations lead to:

- Negative emotions

- Weakened motivation

- Inability to learn or adapt to changes

DEMOTIVATING WORK SITUATIONS

Demotivating work situations similar to those shown below are key contributors to job burnout and can cause even the most motivated person to burnout. In each case, the ingredients required to sustain high motivation are lacking. Check those that apply to your situation.

☐ **THE CRITICAL BOSS.** No matter how hard you try or how well you do, this boss always finds a nit to pick. Eventually, you feel helpless to satisfy this boss.

☐ **BEING A PERFECTIONIST.** Perfectionists focus on eliminating imperfection, no matter how small. Only perfection is acceptable and anything less is criticized as inadequate. Being a perfectionist is like having the worst critical boss—inside your head—constantly criticizing your shortcomings.

☐ **LACK OF RECOGNITION.** Having one's work acknowledged is important, but good work often goes unnoticed. Other forms of lack of recognition include:

　☐ *Inadequate Pay.* When you work hard but feel underpaid, you can feel your efforts and outputs are not being adequately recognized.

　☐ *Underemployment.* If you have high aspirations and spent years in college preparing for work but are employed below your appropriate level, you can equate this with lack of recognition.

DEMOTIVATING WORK SITUATIONS (continued)

☐ **AMBIGUITY.** If you don't know what's expected, it is difficult to feel confident that you are doing the right thing in the right way. Chaotic and ambiguous work situations are common in rapidly expanding high-tech firms. Examples of ambiguity are:

☐ *Lack of Information.* Ambiguity can manifest itself in a lack of enough information to complete your job. As a result you may be working hard on the wrong thing.

☐ *Lack of Clear Goals.* Jobs in rapidly expanding organizations, entrepreneurial operations and poorly managed departments often suffer from lack of clear goals. Without clear goals, you have no target to aim at and little means to determine success.

☐ **TASKS WITHOUT END.** This is the in-basket that is always full; the unending line of customers; assembly line work. This is any job that is repetitive and has no natural beginning and ending point.

Full In-Basket

☐ **IMPOSSIBLE TASKS.** Many people are given assignments that are impossible to achieve. Sometimes the company puts barriers to your accomplishing your assignments. Sometimes the expectations you operate under are impossible to fulfill. In other cases the problem is far beyond the scope of what anyone could possibly achieve, such as expecting police officers to stop all crime. Another common example is the incurable client.

☐ *Incurable Clients.* Many helping professionals have large caseloads of clients with nearly impossible problems.

☐ **NO-WIN SITUATIONS.** There are jobs where, no matter what you do, someone is dissatisfied. Some examples are:

☐ *Incompatible Demands.* If you report to more than one boss, you can be confronted with incompatible demands. One boss may want speed, while another wants quality. Producing both may not be possible. Jobs that require working across departmental boundaries are also plagued by incompatible demands.

☐ *Conflicting Roles.* This can be the woman executive who is expected to be supermom, superwife and star employee—or a manager whose company expects her to travel and whose family wants her at home.

☐ *Value Conflicts.* If you work in a sensitive field such as police work, IRS investigations, military, weapons research or nuclear power, you may face value conflicts. You believe in what you are doing and you strive to do a good job, yet everywhere you go people criticize you for the work you do.

DEMOTIVATING WORK SITUATIONS
(continued)

☐ **BUREAUCRACY.** Traditionally organizations have been built upon the pyramid model with the power at the top and the labor at the bottom. This structure helped organizations to survive by minimizing the power of individuals. Yet, for individuals, powerlessness demotivates and eventually kills the spirit. To maintain motivation, individuals must have power. That is the capacity to influence what happens to oneself and others. People working in certain positions experience more powerlessness than others. These include:

  ☐ *Operations.* More than in other positions, output of operations workers is easy to see and count. Number of errors and accidents, speed of response, quality of output and so forth are counted and compared to specific standards. But at the same time, operations workers are likely to feel frustrated by vague goals and objectives set by supervisors who are poorly trained and ignorant of the technology.

  ☐ *Middle Management.* Generally managers, as compared to operations people, are less susceptible to burnout because their decision-making power gives them more influence over their situations. But not all managers are equally protected. Middle managers are often caught in a psychic squeeze between the incompatible demands of those above and below.

☐ **WORK OVERLOAD.** A lot of work in and of itself is not demotivating as long as you feel you can control what happens and you receive adequate wins. You may be very tired, but motivation can remain high. An *overload of work,* however, is a set-up for job burnout.

☐ **SKILL DEFICIT.** When you don't have the skills needed to perform well and succeed, you can feel helpless. In today's rapidly changing workplace many people are facing new demands—ones that require skills they don't have. Computer literacy is one example.

☐ **MEANINGLESSNESS.** There is a deep human yearning to make a difference. We want to know that our lives mean something and that there is an important purpose in what we do. But the importance of some work is not always apparent, and many people don't know how to find purpose in their work. Without meaningful purpose, work can become a matter of just putting in time.

What Is the Burnout Potential of Your Job?

Now that you have read and reacted to demotivating work situations, it is time to evaluate the burnout potential of your job. Using the scale below, rate how often the situations bother you at work. When finished, add up the ratings to get your score.

| Rarely | 1 | 2 | 3 | 4 | 5 | 6 | 7 | 8 | 9 | Constantly |

POWERLESSNESS

_____ **1.** I can't solve the problems assigned to me.

_____ **2.** I am trapped in my job with no options.

_____ **3.** I am unable to influence decisions that affect me.

_____ **4.** I may be laid off, and there is nothing I can do about it.

INADEQUATE INFORMATION

_____ **5.** I am unclear on the scope and responsibilities of my job.

_____ **6.** I don't have information I need to perform well.

_____ **7.** People I work with don't understand my role.

_____ **8.** I don't understand the purpose of my work.

CONFLICT

_____ **9.** I am caught in the middle.

_____ **10.** I must satisfy conflicting demands.

_____ **11.** I disagree with people at work.

_____ **12.** I must violate procedures in order to get my job done.

POOR TEAM WORK

_____ **13.** Co-workers undermine me.

_____ **14.** Management displays favoritism.

_____ **15.** Office politics interfere with my doing my job.

_____ **16.** People compete instead of cooperate.

WHAT IS THE BURNOUT POTENTIAL OF YOUR JOB? (continued)

Rarely 1   2   3   4   5   6   7   8   9   Constantly

OVERLOAD

_____ **17.** My job interferes with my personal life.

_____ **18.** I have too much to do and too little time to do it.

_____ **19.** I must work on my own time.

_____ **20.** The amount of work I have interferes with how well I do it.

BOREDOM

_____ **21.** I have too little to do.

_____ **22.** I am overqualified for the work I actually do.

_____ **23.** My work is not challenging.

_____ **24.** The majority of my time is spent on routine tasks.

POOR FEEDBACK

_____ **25.** I don't know what I am doing right or what I am doing wrong.

_____ **26.** I don't know what my supervisor thinks of my performance.

_____ **27.** I get information too late to act on it.

_____ **28.** I don't see the results of my work.

PUNISHMENT

_____ **29.** My supervisor is critical.

_____ **30.** Someone else gets credit for my work.

_____ **31.** My work is unappreciated.

_____ **32.** I get blamed for others' mistakes.

ALIENATION

_____ **33.** I am isolated from others.

_____ **34.** I am just a cog in the organizational wheel.

_____ **35.** I don't have much in common with the people I work with.

_____ **36.** I avoid telling people where I work or what I do.

AMBIGUITY

_____ **37.** The rules are constantly changing.

_____ **38.** I don't know what is expected of me.

_____ **39.** There is no relationship between my performance and my success.

_____ **40.** Priorities I must meet are unclear.

UNREWARDING

_____ **41.** My work is not satisfying.

_____ **42.** I have few real successes.

_____ **43.** My career progress is not what I'd hoped.

_____ **44.** I don't get respect.

VALUE CONFLICT

_____ **45.** I must compromise my values.

_____ **46.** People disapprove of what I do.

_____ **47.** I don't believe in the company.

_____ **48.** My heart is not in my work.

_____ **Total**

Scoring:	48–168	Low: Take preventative action.
	169–312	Moderate: Develop a plan to correct problem areas.
	313–432	High: Corrective action is vital.

This test is reprinted by permission from *Beating Job Burnout: How Transform Work Pressure Into Productivity*, Dr. Beverly Potter, Ronin Publishing, © 1993: Beverly A. Potter.

INCREASING MOTIVATION THROUGH PERSONAL POWER

The antidote for burnout is personal power *or a feeling of "I can do," a belief that you can act to control your work.*

When you feel you have no control over events in your life, motivation to continue performing decreases and burnout results. Personal power, skills that render you in control of yourself and what happens to you, insulates you from the negative effects of many work situations. You feel in command. You become a winner because you can make a plan of action and carry it out. You refuel yourself with a sense of accomplishment and other "wins" independent of your boss or the organization.

Making the decision to take command and direct your life is the first and most difficult step to developing personal power. It is here that you may waver. Rebelling against control may be so much a part of you that when you start to take command of yourself, you rebel blindly. This can start a pattern of self-punishment, which confirms your fears of being controlled.

FOLLOW THE EIGHT PATHS TO PERSONAL POWER

PATHS TO PERSONAL POWER

There are eight paths to personal power, all of which will be discussed in detail through the remainder of this book. The paths that you can take to achieve personal power are:

Setting Off on the Path to Power

► Managing Yourself: The First Path

Effective self-management requires knowledge and skill. You probably acquired your self-managing skills informally, from parents and teachers. Consequently, you may not manage yourself effectively. Properly done, self-management increases your personal power because you can create situations in which you can give yourself the "wins" you need to sustain high motivation.

► Managing Stress: The Second Path

It is important to know how your body and mind function and which situations trigger your stress responses. This understanding can be used to raise and lower your tension level as needed. Personal power comes in knowing that, although you may not like the difficult situations, you *can* handle them. Such feelings enable you to rise to the occasion and to handle difficulties skillfully rather than by avoiding problem situations.

► Building Social Support: The Third Path

A strong social support system made up of family, friends and co-workers can help buffer you against the negative effects of stress. People with strong social-support systems tend to be healthier and live longer. It's vitally important that you take active measures to build and maintain your support system.

PATHS TO PERSONAL POWER (continued)

► Skill Building: The Fourth Path

Inevitably, you will encounter situations requiring skills you have not yet developed. Personal power comes from knowing how to arrange learning situations for yourself. When you know how to acquire the skills you need, you'll have confidence to tackle new challenges and handle the unexpected.

► Tailoring the Job: The Fifth Path

Almost every job has some leeway for tailoring it to better fit your work style. The ability to mesh a job to your style increases feelings of potency and enjoyment of work.

► Changing Jobs: The Sixth Path

Sometimes the best solution is to change jobs. Too often, however, burnout victims quit an unsatisfactory job without analyzing the source of dissatisfaction or exploring what is needed, and grab the next job that comes along. Sometimes the new job is as bad as—or even worse—than the old one. Personal power comes in knowing what you need in a job and how to go out and get it.

► Thinking Powerfully: The Seventh Path

Sometimes your emotions may seem out of your control. If so, you may be a victim of runaway thinking. Not knowing how to curb your thoughts, you respond to every red flag waved before you. Personal power comes in knowing how to empty your mind of negative chatter so that you can focus on the moment and the challenges at hand.

► Detached Concern: The Eighth Path

Detached concern is a form of mental control in which personal power is gained by letting go. This is particularly important for those who work with people having serious or even impossible problems. This attachment to your ideas of *how things ought to be* can imprison you and make you feel helpless. As with the Chinese finger puzzle, it's only when you stop pulling and instead push your fingers further into the holder that you can break loose.

MANAGING YOURSELF: THE FIRST PATH TO PERSONAL POWER

Set Yourself Up to Win and Make Getting There Fun!

Self-Management

The way you manage yourself has a direct impact on your motivation and job satisfaction. Good self-managers enjoy working because they get more done and give themselves more credit.

If you use threats and criticism to make yourself work, or if you procrastinate or demand perfection, you are probably far less productive than you could be. You can increase the quality of your work and perform better by improving your self-management abilities.

Managing yourself is not a matter of will power; rather it is an array of simple but effective techniques such as:

- Breaking big jobs down into manageable steps

- Patting yourself on the back

- Indulging yourself for work well done

- Using fun work to reward dull work

Tools to help improve your self-management include:

- Goals

- Objectives

- Want List

- Acknowledging thoughts

- Self-contracts

PERSONAL GOAL SETTING

Suppose you were learning archery but didn't have a target, so you just practiced by shooting into the air. How successful would you be in becoming skilled in archery? Chances are your progress would be slow. You need a target to shoot for. A goal provides such a target by giving you something to aim at.

Goals can help you make decisions. Each day you encounter choices or forks in the road. When you have a goal, it is easier to know which path to take. In this way, goals act as beacons pointing the way. Without goals, you can go around and around, never getting where you want to go. Once you achieve a goal, it is important to set another one. Certain elements increase your chances of meeting a goal:

#1 Be Positive

State what you want to do in terms of a positive action. If you want to avoid or *stop doing something*, state your goals in terms of what you want *to do* instead.

#2 Set a Deadline

Deadlines help you to bring the pieces together. Goals with no specific completion time encourage procrastination and undermine motivation. But a deadline must be realistic if the goal is to be a motivator. Unrealistically short deadlines can trigger panic and generate burnout.

#3 Be Specific

Suppose you have a target, but you can't see where your arrow hits. Your shooting skill would develop very slowly. You need to see where the last shot went so that you can adjust your next shot. This feedback helps you measure your progress towards the goal. Measurability helps determine whether or not you have achieved your goal. The more specific your goal, the easier it is to measure your progress.

#4 Create a Compelling Image

Not all goals are equal. Some are dull, boring and have a repelling effect. Others have a magnetic force that pulls you toward them, creating a target that is easier to hit. A magnetic goal generates a compelling image or picture in your mind when you think about the goal. Can you see yourself accomplishing your goal— and how would you feel?

Go to the Doing Level

A specific goal describes what the accomplished goal will look like. Describe your goal on the *doing level.* Describe what you will be doing (feeling? saying? having? thinking?) when you achieve the goal. Your goal statement should answer the following questions:

- Who is involved?

- What will I be doing?

- When?

- Where (in what circumstances)?

- To what extent? (Under what conditions? To what degree? How much? How long? How hard? etc.)

GOAL SETTING STRATEGIES AHEAD

PERSONAL GOAL SETTING (continued)

Set Better Goals

Remember that to be effective, goals should be positive, have a deadline, be specifically stated and create a compelling image. Consider how closely the following goal statement meets these criteria.

* * *

POOR: *I will stop fighting with people in my department.*

This goal statement violates all of the guidelines. It is negative, stating only what you want to stop doing. There is no deadline. It is not specific and the image it creates is confusing because you don't know what "not fighting" looks like.

* * *

POOR: *I will improve my relationships at work.*

This goal is stated positively. However, it violates the other guidelines. What does an improved relationship look like? How will you recognize it? What will you be doing when relationships are "improved" are not specified. Finally, there is no deadline.

* * *

BETTER: *By the beginning of the year, I will enjoy socializing with co-workers during off hours at least once a month.*

There is a deadline and the goal statement is specific. It will be easier to achieve this goal because you know what to do and when you have done it. An "improved relationship" has been defined in terms of what you will be doing—enjoying socializing. The better goal specifies how much socializing you will do—at least once a month—and when you will do it—after hours. Finally, seeing yourself enjoying socializing is more compelling than imagining "not fighting," which is vague and may bring up uncomfortable images of "giving in" or of "taking it."

Let's try another one.

POOR: *I will improve my time management at work by September 1st.*

This goal is stated positively and there is a deadline. But it is still poorly stated because we don't know the actions involved. What you will be doing when you achieve the goal is vague. This makes it hard to know where to start and difficult to determine if and when the goal has been achieved.

"Time management" can be made more specific if you ask yourself: "What will I be doing when I've improved my time management?" Here are some examples:

* * *

BETTER: *By January 1, I will be able to satisfactorily complete all of my assignments and work at least one hour per day on discretionary projects.*

BETTER: *By Christmas, I will manage my time in such a way that I fly my kite at least two weekday evenings each week.*

Both better goals have deadlines and are specific in describing the goal state— *what you will be doing*—when you achieve the goal (working on discretionary projects and flying your kite). The statements also show how often—at least one hour per day and two weekday evenings—you will be doing the activity when you've improved your management of time. The better goals also create a compelling image in your mind (assuming you enjoy working on discretionary projects and kite flying) because an image of you doing something you like draws you toward it like a magnet.

Setting powerful goals sounds easy, but can be surprisingly difficult. The following worksheet will help you think through your goal so that it is powerful and compelling.

EXERCISE: *Goal Setting*

Step 1: Define My Goal

Write a goal statement that contains the four elements of a powerful goal. Make sure that the goal-statement is (1) positive, (2) has a deadline, (3) is specific and (4) has a compelling image.

My goal is to _____

_____

_____

_____

_____

Step 2: Find the Heart of My Goal

Imagine a time in the future when you've achieved your goal. This is the "goal state." About the goal state, ask yourself, "What do I love about this?" and "What about this goal really matters to me?" Don't try to force an answer. Instead be receptive and notice what thoughts occur and what images come to mind. To these thoughts and images, ask again, "What do I love about this?" and "What about this really matters to me?" Continue exploring your feelings about the goal state until you feel you've come to the heart or essential attraction of the goal. Write the thoughts and images that came to you in the space below.

What I love about the goal. What really matters to me about achieving this: _____

_____

_____

What do the things that matter have in common? _____

_____

_____

Step 3: Observe the **Doing** *of the Goal State*

Close your eyes and breathe deeply until you feel calm and relaxed. Now *imagine yourself in the goal state*—that time in the future when you have achieved your goal. Don't worry about *how* you'll achieve the goal, just imagine the time when the goal has been achieved. What does the goal state look like? What are you doing? Look for actions and outcomes. What are others doing? What resources are used? What money? What people are involved? What technology? Just study the details of the goal state. List anything you saw when imagining the goal state—especially anything that you didn't expect. Finally, describe how you *felt* when imagining yourself in the goal state.

List the specific behaviors and outcomes that occur when the goal is achieved: _____

_____

_____

What did you see that you didn't expect? _____

_____

_____

How did you feel when in the goal state? _____

_____

_____

Step 4: Refine My Goal

Revise your goal statement to make it more compelling. Use what you observed when you pictured the goal state to revise the target you are shooting for. Make it even more attractive. Remember to focus on the heart of the goal, what really matters.

My compelling goal is to _____

_____

_____

Picture Your Goal Often! Imagine yourself in the goal state every day if you can. Add details to your image of the completed goal. The more clear and positive your picture is, the more compelling and powerful your goal will be.

ACCOMPLISHING YOUR GOALS THROUGH SMALL STEPS

The word "Inertia" means that a body at rest tends to stay at rest, while a body in motion tends to stay in motion.

Imagine that your car has a dead battery and you must push it to get it started. The greatest effort to get the car moving is the first push. This is when you break the inertia and move the car from rest to motion. Once moving, it takes much less effort to keep the car moving.

If you are like many people, you often have trouble getting started toward your goal. The problem is inertia. You are a body at rest! You must break the inertia to get moving.

The secret to getting started is to take small steps. The secret to keeping momentum is to take small steps.

Taking Small Steps

Setting Objectives

Objectives are tools for making the steps needed to achieve your goal. An objective is a *precise statement of what you plan to do during each step.* Objectives can be thought of as milestones along the path to your goal. Objectives that meet the following guidelines are easier to achieve.

Set Yourself Up to Win

Your small step should be only as big as what you *know* you can achieve with relative ease. If it is something difficult—because it is distasteful or involves an entrenched habit—then shorten the time frame of the first small objective. For example, suppose you want to stop smoking. If, for your first objective, you demand that for a month you will chew gum every time you feel like smoking, you are likely to fail. Chances for success are better if you make the first objective for one day instead. When you meet that objective, set another one for a slightly longer period of time. Set objectives that you *know you can meet*. Set yourself up to succeed. The objective helps you get started and creates momentum. Once you've broken the inertia of a bad habit, you have also started to develop a winner's attitude. This, too, will help you to succeed.

Stretch Yourself

Although objectives should be small steps, they should be big enough to make you stretch. Think of yoga as an example. When doing yoga, you position your body in a posture and then slowly s t r e t c h the muscles you are exercising. Don't worry about the steps being too small as long as there is some stretch and some movement. Remember the inertia principle: "A body in motion tends to stay in motion." Use small steps to keep yourself in motion toward your goal.

Make Getting There Fun

People often equate self-management or self-discipline with austerity—sacrifice and no pleasure. Such an approach is a mistake and will undermine your success. Grease the wheels of change with fun. Enjoyment of a task lessens the toil of doing it. Consider physical exercise. Doing jumping jacks and running in place isn't much fun. By comparison, playing tennis with a friend is more fun. And it provides a good workout. With this in mind, think of ways you can build fun into the process of achieving your goals.

HOW TO SET OBJECTIVES

Begin by identifying the steps to your goal. Next, this section will teach you how to arrange the steps into a map. Finally, you will learn to describe the *what* and *when* of reaching each step with objectives.

Identify Steps and Create a Map

There are several ways to identify steps to your goal. One of the most effective is to begin at the end, with your goal completed, and work backward through the steps needed to achieve your goal.

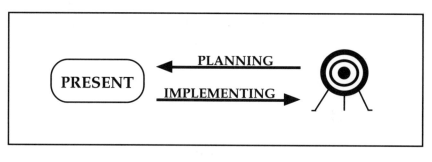

Begin at the End

Begin at the End

Imagine the goal state, the time when the goal has been achieved. Ask yourself "Can I do this now?" If the answer is "No," ask, "What step must I do first?" Then imagine that step completed and ask, "Can I do this now? If not, what step must I do first?" Continue this questioning process with each step identified until you get to a step that you can do *now*.

Create a Map

A journey of a thousand miles begins with the first step. Similarly, you reach your goal by beginning with what you can do now. In the next section, you will create a map of the steps to your goal.

CASE STUDY: *Janice's Map*

PART 1: Janice's goal was to set up an on-line database of health-care trends. To figure out the steps to her goal, she began at the end by asking, "Can I do this now?" The answer was "No." So Janice asked, "What do I have to do before I can set up the database?" She saw that the data had to be input first. Look at the following illustration and you will see that for the first step backward, Janice drew a circle to the left of her goal and wrote "input data" in it.

With one step identified, Janice repeated the process by asking "Can I input the data now?" Again the answer was "no." Thinking of what she had to do before inputting data, she identified "gather data" as the next step backward. When Janice wondered if gathering the data could be done now, she realized that two steps had to be completed first. The database had to be designed, but before she could do that she had to collect studies and product information. This was needed to identify the kind of information that would go in the database. To collect studies and product information, Janice decided she would have to poll industry experts and that she needed to first identify experts to poll. Identifying experts is something she *can* do immediately. Janice had followed the steps going backward from "gathering data" until she got to a step she can do now.

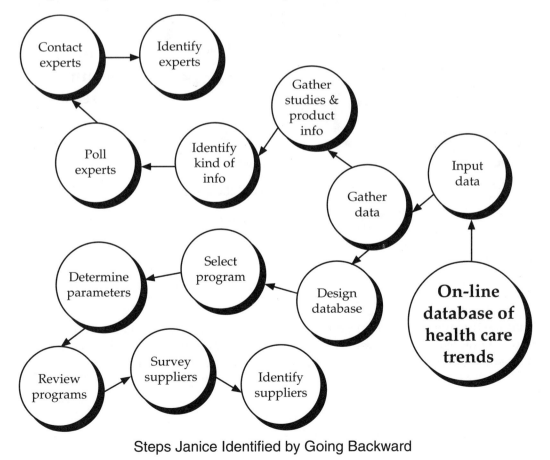

Steps Janice Identified by Going Backward

CASE STUDY (continued)

PART 2: After identifying the steps backward from her goal, each of the activities became action steps. With this process she created a map for getting to her goal.

Steps Forward to Janice's Goal

Taking Steps to My Goal

My Goal: _____

_____

Imagine the goal state when your goal has been completed and ask, "Can I do this now? If not, What step must I do first?" Ask the same question of that step and each subsequent step until you get to a step you can do now. List the steps below.

Steps: _____

_____

Determining Small Steps

Take each step you just identified and break it down into several small steps. List the small steps. Put a check next to an easy small step you can start with. If you wonder if you could actually take this small step, break it into even smaller steps and choose an easy one to begin with.

Smaller Steps: _____

_____

_____

_____

_____

Create Your Map

Write your goal in the target at the right. Ask of the goal, "Can I do this now?" If the answer is "No," ask, "What do I have to do first?" Write this in the first circle to the left of your goal. Of this step and each subsequent step, ask those two questions. When you've identified all of the steps, fill in the steps on the map.

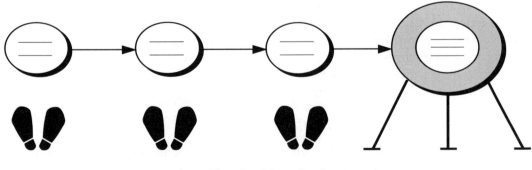

Mapping Your Goals

DEFINE OBJECTIVES BY THE RESULTS YOU WILL ACHIEVE

An objective is a step along your path to your destination. Effective objectives are defined by the results that come when you reach them. By concentrating on results, you can evaluate whether or not you've completed the step. Set an objective for each step to your goal.

An Objective

- Describes a result that will exist when it is achieved

- Is measurable and attainable

- And has a completion date

A Good Objective States What Will Be Achieved—But Not How

An objective describes a result that you will achieve for each step toward your goal. A result is an outcome. It describes what you aim to achieve, but not how you will do so. *How* refers to an activity or process. *Activities* are things you do to achieve a result.

A Good Objective Is Measurable

Measurability tells you when you've completed each step. For instance, long-distance runners aiming for a ten-mile marker would have difficulty telling when they reached it without a mileage counter. Measurability also lets you know how close you are to completing each step. It has a bolstering effect that builds confidence and feelings of control. These feelings, in turn, promote personal power and help prevent burnout.

A Good Objective Is Attainable

Objectives that make you stretch a little are good, but objectives that you cannot attain are frustrating and diminish motivation. Remember, you want to gain confidence and boost your motivation. Instead of demanding a giant step, set a series of goals that will stretch you enough to make you feel good about yourself, but avoid demanding the impossible of yourself.

A Good Objective Has a Completion Date

A completion date provides a clear point in time to achieve the result. Like the other elements of an objective, the completion date can be motivating if it is realistic or discouraging if it is unrealistic. The completion date enables you to schedule activities and to pace yourself. If you fall behind, the completion date reveals this quickly so that you can take corrective action before things get hopeless.

Milestones

The Result I Will Achieve

Specify one of the major milestones or steps toward your goal. Then describe the outcome or result that will be achieved when you reach that step. Remember that a result is an end point and not an activity or process.

STEP: Describe a step you have identified that is necessary to your goal. _____

_____

_____

RESULT: Describe the outcome that will be achieved when you complete that step. _____

_____

_____

DEFINE OBJECTIVES BY THE RESULTS YOU WILL ACHIEVE (continued)

Identify My Objective

Write a detailed objective for the first step on the way to your goal. Remember an objective is a statement of the result or outcome that you will achieve. A well-stated objective has a completion date, is attainable and can be measured.

My Objective: _____

_____

_____

_____

_____

Giving Yourself "Wins" for Successes

Giving yourself acknowledgment and rewards for what you've done provides the motivational "wins" necessary to keep taking steps toward your goal. Poor self-managers tend to do just the opposite. They focus on their failures and criticize what they did wrong. Self-criticism tends to set up a vicious cycle of "working to avoid," in which work is done to avoid guilt and anxious feelings. Self-acknowledgment, on the other hand, promotes "working for." It stimulates much better feelings.

Acknowledgment can be expressed in a variety of ways, such as by giving yourself things you want, by allowing yourself to do things you enjoy, or by giving yourself or letting others give you praise for things you've done well. Begin by identifying things you want and what you enjoy doing.

My Want List

Make a list of things you like doing and things you want. Include activities and social encounters you enjoy and things you want to continue doing. Give yourself items from your Want List as rewards for meeting your small-step objectives. These are pleasures you have earned!

Things I Like Doing	Things I Want
_____	_____
_____	_____
_____	_____
_____	_____
_____	_____
_____	_____
_____	_____
_____	_____

"Most Wanted" List

PUT TOGETHER A PLAN OF ACTION

Decide (1) what small step you will take, (2) what reward you will give yourself as a "win" for doing it and (3) what acknowledging thought you can think about your accomplishment.

My Action Plan

Review your list of small steps and select a few easy first steps. Describe them below. Review your Want List and select a reward you will give yourself as a "win." In the third column write a positive statement you can think to yourself about having successfully completed the step.

Small Step	Want List	Acknowledgments
_____	_____	_____
_____	_____	_____
_____	_____	_____
_____	_____	_____
_____	_____	_____
_____	_____	_____
_____	_____	_____
_____	_____	_____

The Self-Contract

Using a New Year's resolution can sabotage your good intentions. In this all-or-nothing approach you resolve to never again do whatever it is that you want to stop doing or to always do something you want to do. One transgression and you have failed. "Always" and "never" are impossible standards to meet.

On the other hand, the self-contract is a powerful tool for climbing the small steps to success. A self-contract is a written agreement that you make with yourself specifying each small-step objective you intend to carry out, the "win" you will give yourself for doing it, and what you will say to yourself to acknowledge your accomplishment. A self-contract, like all contracts, has a term that states how long the agreement will last. Self-contract terms can be for a few days or for weeks, months or years.

Write a contract for only as much change as you know you can accomplish. Be sure that the time frame is short enough so that you know you can stick to your resolve. This is important. When the contract is fulfilled, give yourself a reward or a "win" and acknowledge your accomplishment. Then move to the next step. Increase the amount, intensity or quality of your performance—or the length of the contract. Successfully completed contracts are "wins" that fuel motivation.

The contract is a tool to get you into motion and keep you in motion. It is a way of teaching yourself to "work for" and to develop enthusiasm for work. Use the self-contract on page 44.

Summary of Self-Management

Remember, self-management is the first path to personal power. Effective self-management skills increase personal power and help prevent job burnout. When you can accomplish what you set out to do, you feel strong and in control of your job and your life. Self-management is the first path because you need it to follow the other seven paths to personal power.

NOW ... FILL IN THE SELF-CONTRACT ON THE NEXT PAGE

SELF-CONTRACT

I will *(describe small step)* _____

_____

_____

When I complete this I will reward myself with *(item from Want List)*

_____

_____

_____

I will acknowledge myself by thinking *(positive statement)* _____

_____

_____

I will do this by *(date or term of contract)* _____

_____

_____

Date _____ Signature _____

MANAGING STRESS: THE SECOND PATH TO PERSONAL POWER

Stress Is the Fever of Burnout. And Like a Fever, You Must Bring the Stress Down to Preserve Your Health.

Stress is the fever of burnout! If you had pneumonia it would be essential to keep the accompanying fever down to avoid brain damage. But bringing down a fever will not cure pneumonia. The same is true with the stress that accompanies burnout. You must bring the stress down to preserve health, but reducing stress will not eliminate the underlying cause of burnout, which is a feeling of powerlessness.

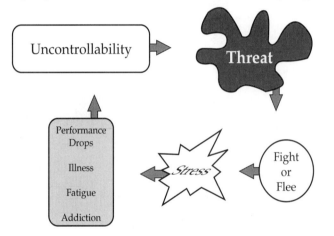

How Burnout Is Stressful

Following are some principles that explain what is known about the stress cycle.

1. **Loss of Control = Threat.** One of the most serious threats we can encounter is uncontrollability. All animals, especially human beings, are concerned about controlling their respective worlds. Striving to control the world around us is a survival drive. When we feel a loss of control, we feel threatened, and this triggers the "fight-flight" response.

2. **Fight-Flight.** When confronted with threat, a body mobilizes to either fight the threat or flee from it. Muscles tense, blood rushes and breathing quickens. But when you neither fight nor flee, but remain in the powerless situation, the result is chronic stress.

3. **Chronic Stress.** It is this unrelenting chronic stress that causes many of the symptoms of burnout. Some are exhaustion, health problems, irritability, intellectual impairment and emotional outbursts—which is why stress must be treated.

OBJECTIVE OF STRESS MANAGEMENT

The objective of stress management is to keep stress or tension levels within the optimal range for performance, health and well-being.

At *high* levels of stress, performance is low because stress impairs physical and intellectual functioning. In this state it feels as if you are spinning your wheels. High stress interferes with creative performance and may be manifested by hyperactivity, forgetfulness, frequent mistakes, lack of concentration, or irritability. Unrelenting high stress can damage your health.

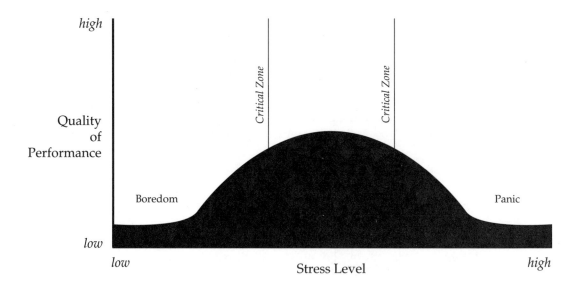

When overstimulated, you must try to *reduce your tension* level to bring it back down to the ideal range. Place a checkmark by activities as you use them.

☐ meditate

☐ breathe deeply

☐ systematically relax your muscles

☐ imagine a relaxing scene

☐ listen to slow, melodic music

☐ take a day off

☐ watch fish swim in an aquarium

☐ take a warm bath

☐ lie on a soft bed

☐ eat bland food

☐ drink warm milk or herbal tea

☐ take a stroll

When stress is very low, performance tends to be low as well. There is too little stimulation to keep attention on what is at hand. This is called boredom, or in the extreme, depression.

When bored, depressed or doing routine work, try to *raise your tension* level to bring it up to the optimal range. Place a checkmark by activities as you use them.

☐ look for problems to solve   ☐ eat spicy food

☐ take a cold shower   ☐ listen to upbeat music

☐ exercise   ☐ work in a peopled area

These stimulating activities will increase tension level and help you move into the ideal range for performing.

Stress-Management Can Become Urgent

TO FIND OUT WHY, READ ON . . .

OBJECTIVE OF STRESS MANAGEMENT (continued)

Controlling Stress

The first step to controlling stress is to identify situations that stress you and gather information on how you respond to them. Then you can see your response habits and develop a plan for change.

Create a Personal Stress Log

Each time you feel angry, upset, pressured, anxious, excited, worried or frustrated, stop and look at yourself and the situation. Create a stress log similar to the one shown below and note the following data:

1. *When did the event occur? What day and time?*

2. *What was the situation? Who was there? Where did it happen?*

3. *Rate your distress level, using a scale from 1 to 10, with 1 being "very little distress" and 10 being "extremely upset."*

4. *How did you respond? What were your thoughts? How did you feel? What did you do?*

My Personal Stress Log

When	Situation	Distress Level	Response: Thoughts, Feelings and Actions
_____	_____	_____	_____
_____	_____	_____	_____
_____	_____	_____	_____
_____	_____	_____	_____
_____	_____	_____	_____

DISCOVER YOUR PERSONAL STRESS PATTERNS

Collect data on your stress responses for several days. Then review your Personal Stress Log, looking for patterns. What generalizations can you make about the times and situations that were distressing?

► Are deadlines a frequent cause for panic?

► Is there a particular person or type of event that appears several times in your Personal Stress Log?

► What responses do you use over and over?

► Do you eat when you feel anxious?

► Do you avoid certain situations?

Stress Patterns Analysis

Discover stress patterns by analyzing what the situations have in common. From this analysis, you can begin making a plan for managing stress. Are there situations you can avoid? Perhaps you can foresee stressing events and prepare for the encounter? How might you respond more effectively?

Types of Patterns	**My Usual Response**	**Possible Plan of Action**

People

_____   _____   _____

_____   _____   _____

_____   _____   _____

Places

_____   _____   _____

_____   _____   _____

_____   _____   _____

Events

_____   _____   _____

_____   _____   _____

_____   _____   _____

Time

_____   _____   _____

_____   _____   _____

_____   _____   _____

Other: Specify

_____   _____   _____

_____   _____   _____

_____   _____   _____

STRESS REDUCTION TECHNIQUES

There are several ways for a person to reduce your level of stress. These will be discussed in the next few pages. They include learning how to breathe, recognizing tension, exercises to systematically relax muscles, and using your imagination.

Breathing Correctly

It seems crazy to explain the correct way to breathe because we tend to think it is something we do naturally. Yet, many people breathe shallowly so that too much air remains in their lungs.

▶ *Slow Deep Breathing Automatically Relaxes.* Even a few minutes of deep breathing will produce noticeable changes in tension level. Deep breathing can be used any time and any place. Several deep breaths just before a difficult situation is calming and increases feelings of control.

▶ *Learn How to Breathe.* During inhalation the diaphragm contracts and descends. This increases lung capacity. During exhalation the diaphragm relaxes and moves upward, forcing air out. In other words, when you breathe in, your abdomen should go out. When you breathe out, the abdomen should go in.

▶ *Check Your Breathing.* Place your hand on your abdomen and notice what happens when you breathe. Does your hand go out when you inhale and in when you exhale? Hold your hand on your abdomen the first couple of times you do this exercise to make sure you are breathing correctly. As you gain skill and lung capacity, slowly increase the inhale and exhale periods to six seconds, then to eight seconds.

Breath Control Technique

 Inhale slowly and deeply for four seconds, while counting 1-and-2-and-3-and-4. Notice the full feeling in your lungs.

 Exhale slowly for four seconds, while counting 1-and-2-and-3-and-4. Try to push out even more air.

 Repeat steps 1 and 2 while focusing all your attention on breathing and counting until you are able to increase your inhale and exhale periods to eight seconds.

IDENTIFYING TENSION

Learning to relax in difficult situations increases personal power! You can keep tension within the optimal range during a crisis and have all your resources to draw upon. You can be confident that you can stay cool while allowing your body to rest and repair as you prepare for optimal functioning.

Identifying your tension level from moment to moment is the first step. "Oh, I know how tense I am," you may say. "I know when I'm uptight!" This is not always the case. In fact, most people do not accurately read their tension levels and are *not* aware of how inaccurate they can be. When you first become tense, it feels uncomfortable. But the discomfort fades rapidly, making it easy to misread your tension level—and you've missed a vital warning signal.

Experiment One

Procedure	Make a *very tight fist* with your left hand and continue holding it for 60 seconds.
Observe	Like a scientist, objectively study what you feel, where you feel it, and how intensely you feel it.
Procedure	After 60 seconds, make a *very tight fist* with your right hand while continuing to hold your left fist tight.
Observe	What are you experiencing in your right fist? How does this compare to what you feel in your left fist? Notice how tension feels stronger in your right hand than in your left?

With the techniques given here you can train yourself to sense tension in a short time. Start by discriminating between sensations of tension and those of relaxation. Repeat the experiments several times until you become familiar with the sensations of tension and relaxation in the muscles of your hand.

Experiment Two

Procedure	*Lightly tense* your left fist. The degree of tension should be just enough to notice.
Observe	Like a scientist, objectively study what you feel in your fist. For seven to ten seconds focus on exactly where and how the sensation of tension is for you.
Procedure	Create contrast by *quickly opening* your fist to release the tension and consciously relaxing the muscles in your hand.
Observe	Watch what you experience in your left hand. In a detached manner, compare how your hand feels when relaxed with how they feel when tense. Use this as a point of reference.

SYSTEMATICALLY RELAX MUSCLES

It takes about 25 minutes to systematically relax the muscles in your body. Here's how:

Starting with your head and face and *slowly* moving down your body, tense and relax your muscles in the same way that you did with your fist. Hold the tension for seven to ten seconds, except for the feet, which you should hold for only three to four seconds to avoid cramping. Study and compare the sensations of tension and relaxation in each muscle.

► **BREATHING**

Deep breathing helps to relax you. Breathe in during the tensing phase and out during the relaxation phase. (Review the section on breathing if you need to.) Breathe deeply in and out before moving to the next muscle.

► **TALK TO YOURSELF**

Just before you release the tension and exhale, tell yourself to "Relax." Eventually, you will learn to release tension in a particular muscle group by focusing your attention on it and telling yourself to relax. This is a "relax command."

Tense ➡ Observe
Relax ➡ Observe

Compare

Tension vs. Relaxation

As you explore the various facets of personal power, you will see that the essential ingredient is self-observation. To know what stresses you, how you respond, how you think and how you feel requires your observation.

Relaxation

With eyes closed, tense and relax each muscle, one at a time. Study the sensation of tension in the muscle. Think, "Relax," and then release the tension from the muscle, relaxing it as much as you can. Study the sensation of relaxation. Compare the sensations of relaxation and tension.

Face and Throat

Face: Squint eyes, wrinkle nose and try to pull your whole face into a point at the center.

Forehead: Knit or raise eyebrows.

Nose and upper lip: With mouth slightly open, slowly bring upper lip down to lower lip.

Mouth: Bring lips together into a tight point, then press mouth into teeth. Blow out gently to relax.

Lips and tongue: With teeth slightly apart, press lips together and push tongue into top of mouth.

Chin: With arms crossed over chest, stick out your chin and turn it slowly as far as it will go to the left. Repeat for right side.

Neck: Push your chin into your chest at the same time as pushing your head backwards into the back of your chair to create a counter-force.

Arms and Hands

Hands and forearm: Make a fist.

Biceps: Bend the arm at the elbow and make a "he-man" muscle.

Upper Body

Shoulders: Attempt to touch your ears with your shoulders.

Upper back: Push shoulder blades together and stick out chest.

Chest: Take a deep breath and hold it for several seconds.

Stomach: Pull stomach into spine or push it out.

Lower Body

Buttocks: Tighten buttocks and push into chair.

Thighs: Straighten leg and tighten thigh muscles.

Calves: Point toes toward your head.

Toes: Curl toes.

Do this exercise in a quiet, private place and notice when you finish how good it feels to be totally relaxed.

RELAXATION TRAINING PLAN

The next section gives you a plan for action, but first let's start with an analysis of what stressful situations are the most difficult for you.

Distressing Situations

Review the Personal Stress Log you made earlier and list the distressing situations in order, *from the least distressing to the most distressing.* Use the distress level ratings you made at that time.

Distress Rating	Distressing Situations
_____	_____
_____	_____
_____	_____
_____	_____
_____	_____
_____	_____
_____	_____
_____	_____

RELAXATION TRAINING PLAN (continued)

Practice Relaxing

► *A Quiet Spot:* In the beginning it's a good idea to practice in a quiet spot that you already find relaxing. You might try a lawn chair in your backyard, or a comfortable sofa. Your bed is an old stand-by. But don't be surprised if you fall asleep! Answer the following:

"My quiet spot for relaxation practice is _____."

► *At Work:* After practicing in a quiet spot for about two weeks, slowly transfer the practice to your daily routine. The key here is *slowly*.

► *Relax Your Muscles:* Instead of a coffee break, you might close your office door, turn off the lights, and spend five minutes tensing and relaxing muscles. Or you might practice during other times when you are waiting for the elevator, waiting on hold on the telephone or waiting for a meeting to start.

► *Tell Yourself to "Relax":* Use the "Relax" command. Take a deep breath and tell yourself to relax. Bring to mind tension-producing situations, such as riding the bus home from work. This is an ideal way to unwind for the evening. Or try it before making that phone call that you have been putting off.

Creating a Pleasant Fantasy

Tension can be lowered quite rapidly by taking a few breaths and imagining a pleasant fantasy. A pleasant fantasy can be anything positive: a *real situation,* such as lying in a hammock in your backyard, or a *pretend scene,* such as riding on a billowy white cloud. There need be no limits. The only requirement is that imagining it relaxes you.

► *A Special Place:* Your pleasant fantasy is a special place you can visit at any time and in any situation to relax and refuel. Just a three-to-four-minute visit will have a rejuvenating effect.

► *Visit Often:* Visit your pleasant fantasy just before a difficult situation, to take a break from demanding work, or to prepare for a change in activity.

A Pleasant Way to Control Stress

Scripting Your Pleasant Fantasy

Write a description of a situation you find particularly relaxing. Add as much detail as you can. The more the scene stimulates your senses, the more powerful it will be in relaxing you.

Where I will be: _____

What I will see: _____

What I will hear: _____

What I will feel: _____

What I will smell: _____

Wiggle yourself into a comfortable spot and loosen your belt and shoes. With your eyes closed, breathe deeply to relax yourself. Imagine yourself in your pleasant fantasy. Imagine all the details you wrote on paper. Bring it to life, making it as vivid as possible. Think about the details. Imagine with all your senses. Your pleasant fantasy may come more strongly through some of the senses than others. Don't worry about this. With practice your ability to imagine will improve. Don't look at yourself as a character on a TV screen. Instead *put yourself into the situation.* Imagine yourself *inside* your body during the scene. Notice new sights, smells, sounds, sensations, and tastes that you didn't write on the paper. After returning from your pleasant fantasy, add these new discoveries to the description of your scene:

Where I was: _____

What I saw: _____

What I heard: _____

What I felt: _____

What I smelled: _____

CHANGING YOUR ENVIRONMENT

Environments have the power to stimulate us in different ways. Some environments are relaxing while others are filled with stressors. The more uncertain the environment, the more it contains the possibility of danger. Uncertainty is a stressor. Environments with a lot of information to be processed are also stressing. Because we don't know what's out there, all the senses must operate. We mobilize into alertness, the optimal level to process information. The amount of uncertainty and information in the environment is called *load*. By changing *environmental load*, you can increase or decrease your tension level.

ENVIRONMENTAL LOAD	
High Load	**Low Load**
Uncertain	Certain
Unknown	Known
Irregular	Regular
Newness	Redundancy

How to Use Load to Manage Stress

The objective with stress management is to keep your tension level in the optimal range for performance. Looking back to the graph on page 47 you can see that the optimal level is the high point of the bell curve and as your tension level goes up or down, the quality of your performance declines.

When you are very tense or "stressed out" you need to *bring your tension level down* to keep in the optimal range. On the other hand, when you are bored or depressed your tension level is too low to perform optimally, and you need to take action to *increase your tension.*

▶ *Music*

You can alter mood faster with music than with drugs. Compare how you feel listening to rock and roll with how you feel listening to a church hymn. We respond physically and emotionally within seconds to music. Not only do we respond to the rhythm, but music also brings up memories that are usually accompanied with emotions.

► *Color and Design*

Soft, muted colors and regular designs are low load and have a calming effect. Bright colors such as reds, yellows, oranges and bold designs in clashing colors are high load and stimulating.

► *Lighting*

Change mood with colored light bulbs. Use a soft yellow light for meetings to promote relaxation, and a bright white light (which is more stimulating) when doing boring work.

► *People*

People probably have the highest load. Friends can be unpredictable. Groups of people, especially strangers, are high load. You can use this rule to your advantage by taking tedious, repetitive paper work to the cafeteria where the stimulating presence of other people can bring your tension level up. Take difficult work requiring a lot of concentration into a private conference room where the absence of stimulation can help you relax and concentrate.

► *Baths*

Stretching out in a tepid bath is relaxing. When you need to perk up, take a cold shower.

Soak Your Tension Away

CHANGING YOUR ENVIRONMENT (continued)

▶ *Food*

Any kind of spicy or unusual food is stimulating, while bland and familiar foods like mashed potatoes or rice have the opposite effect. Cayenne pepper and ginseng are two natural stimulants. Milk and valerian tea are relaxants.

▶ *Level of Hunger*

A mild degree of hunger is stimulating. You may have noticed how drowsy you get after a large meal, especially in the afternoon. If you must give a speech and are nervous, bring your tension level down by drinking milk and eating pancakes, mashed potatoes, rice, or some other starchy bland food. If you must attend a boring meeting, skip lunch so you are slightly hungry—which is stimulating—and drink a cup of coffee beforehand. Alternatively, eat a hot peppery snack beforehand.

▶ *Exercise*

When you are bored or depressed, vigorous exercise is a good way to pick yourself up. When you are highly stressed, a mild light exercise such as a walk around the block will help release tension so you can relax.

Don't Just Sit There, Exercise!

▶ *Fantasy*

Fantasies about eating wonderful ten-course meals or imagining your pleasant fantasy will relax you when you are very tense. If relaxation is not what you want, use adventuresome or sexual fantasies to perk yourself up.

SELF-CONTRACT FOR MANAGING STRESS

Beginning with the least distressing situation, develop a plan of action for handling the situation. You might use deep breathing when you are in the situation. Or you might work on relaxing the muscles directly while thinking, "Relax." Then write a self-contract for practicing relaxing while in the situation. Remember to acknowledge your successes often. When you can handle the mildest situation and remain relaxed, move to the next situation on the list.

When (*least distressing situation*) _____

_____

I will (*plan for relaxing*) _____

_____

When I have done this I will (*reward from Want List*) _____

_____

This contract will be in effect until (*duty or term of contract*) _____

_____

Date _____ Signature _____

Summary of Stress Management

When you know that you can handle stressful situations, you feel more powerful. Not only will you protect your health, but you are likely to perform better and get more "wins." The increased "wins" and feelings of control help to buffer you against burnout situations at work.

BUILDING SOCIAL SUPPORT: THE THIRD PATH TO PERSONAL POWER

Social Support Acts As a Buffer Against Stress and Burnout!

You can tolerate a greater degree of stress when you have caring and supportive relationships. In fact, research shows that people with close emotional and social ties are physically and mentally healthier and live longer!

Close friends and good relationships with co-workers and family reaffirm your competence and self-worth. They can help to get things done and provide you with valuable information. They can help you handle difficult situations. They can listen to your problems and give feedback. They can help you learn new skills. They can encourage you to tackle challenges and accomplish goals.

It's Healthy to Have Friends

Hints for Building Social Relationships

#1 Communicate Goodwill

Goodwill is communicated through social rituals. It promotes a comfortable ambiance and invites people to speak to you. Say "Hi" or "Good morning" in an upbeat voice and communicate friendliness in your nonverbal gestures. Smile and look at people in an interested way when speaking with them. An open posture, leaning forward, and lightly touching a person's shoulder or arm communicates your receptivity.

#2 Show Interest in Others

The most powerful resource you have for building social relationships is your attention. When you pay attention to others, they feel good about themselves and about you. Showing interest is easy. All you have to do is ask questions. Find out how others feel about community issues. Ask about hobbies. Be curious about what others want to accomplish.

Here are some powerful questions for showing interest:

- What happened?
- What did you do?
- How did you feel?
- What's your opinion?
- What do you suggest?
- What's an example?
- What do you mean?

#3 Invite Others

Don't just wait to be invited. Start inviting others to do things with you. Ask co-workers to join you for lunch. Look through the paper for interesting events and ask a friend to accompany you. People love to be invited out.

#4 Make Others Winners

It's easy to make others winners. All you have to do is notice what a person is doing well and comment on it. It only takes a minute. Try it.

#5 Be Helpful

When you help others accomplish their goals, they are inclined to want to help you, too. Helping doesn't take a lot of effort. Sometimes it is as easy as sharing information. Or you might introduce people to each other. Get outside of yourself and think about what you could do to help someone else. Even if nothing else comes of it, helping feels good.

BUILDING SOCIAL SUPPORT: THE THIRD PATH TO PERSONAL POWER (continued)

#6 Give Information

Information is power. Information helps people get ahead. Be generous with your information. When someone performs better as a result of information from you, that person will be inclined to be more supportive of you.

#7 Ask for Advice

When you ask others for advice, they are flattered. They feel important. And they become committed to you. They want to see you succeed.

#8 Be a Team Player

Work cooperatively with co-workers to accomplish your group's purpose. Being a team player means sometimes setting other people up so they can win. When another person wins and the team advances, everyone wins. You become an important player upon whom others depend.

Team Players

#9 Show Belonging

When you look like you belong, it is easier for people to talk with you because you seem to have something in common. Begin by acting "as if" you belong. Emulate the language style and gestures that members use. Tell group jokes. Use words like "we" and "us." Introduce people to one another like a member would, even if you've just met them yourself.

WAYS TO SHOW BELONGING

Language Style	Slang, intonations, drawls, accents, pronouns "we" and "us," inside jokes, nicknames, stories about the group.
Gestures	Handshakes, hugs, body language, salutes like raised fist, peace symbol, thumbs up.
Clothing	Sports icons like hats, tee-shirts, political ribbons and buttons; Ivy League sporty, cowboy style.
Grooming	Hair styles like crew cuts, tiny pigtails, braids; beards, make-up, jewelry, fancy fingernails.

Building Social Support

Relationships don't develop in a vacuum. You must create them. Think of specific things you can do today to start building your relationships.

What I can do to build my relationships with my family and friends: _____

_____

_____

What I can do to build my relationships with co-workers: _____

_____

_____

What I can do to become involved in professional or social associations: _____

_____

_____

BUILD A NETWORK OF ALLIES

The modern workplace is a social environment. Succeeding on the job requires more than just accomplishing tasks. It also means building allies who can give you needed information, connect you with the right person and open doors to valuable resources. You can improve your effectiveness by taking time to build a network of allies.

Effective people know how to find things out and how to get things done. The most effective people have allies throughout the organization. They cultivate friendly relationships in every division and help others. In turn, they can count on allies to help them.

Build a Network of Allies

How to Network

Networking is a process of making the acquaintance of people who might be able to link you to other people who may be able to help you in various ways.

▶ **Connect With People At All Levels.** Pick potential allies on the basis of the information and resources they have access to rather than their position. Sometimes people in seemingly low positions have useful information.

▶ **Be Generous With Your Support**. Think in terms of what helpful information, advice or contacts you have to give, rather than questioning what you can get from others. People you have helped tend to want to help you in return.

Developing Your Ally Network

Think of every person you know through your work, your family, professional groups, recreations and socially. List those you could approach for information, referrals and advice. Indicate in the second column what kinds of things they know about and what resources they might be able to help you with. Since you know a lot of people, this is a big task. Don't try to remember everyone all at once. Instead, come back to this list often and jot down names as they come to you. The resulting list is your Ally Network, one of the major resources you have for making your projects succeed.

Ally

**What They Know
(or resources they control)**

Work: Clients, colleagues and their friends, associates and acquaintances

_____   _____

_____   _____

Family: Relatives and their friends, acquaintances and business associates

_____   _____

_____   _____

Professional Groups: Associates and their friends and acquaintances

_____   _____

_____   _____

Recreational Groups: Members and their friends, associates and acquaintances

_____   _____

_____   _____

Social: Current and old friends, their friends and associates—even people where you shop, worship, have your hair done, and so on

_____   _____

_____   _____

Who I Have Helped, Who I Can Help

Think back over the last couple of months and recall people you have helped. Think of "help" in broad terms to include giving helpful information, providing access to resources and people, giving referrals, and backing up people's ideas. Include people from all levels—at work, from professional associations and in your personal life. List these people below, indicating how you helped them and how they might help you. Next, list people you might be able to help. Indicate how you might help them and ways in which they might help you. When you need support, look over this list and see if there is someone you have helped whom you could call upon.

People I Have Helped Recently

Who	*How I Helped*	*How He or She Could Help Me*
_____	_____	_____
_____	_____	_____
_____	_____	_____
_____	_____	_____
_____	_____	_____

People I Could Help

Who	*How I Could Help*	*How He or She Could Help Me*
_____	_____	_____
_____	_____	_____
_____	_____	_____
_____	_____	_____

► **Know What You Need.** It is difficult to communicate what you need if you don't know what it is. And how will you know when you've gotten it? Take the time to think through what information, advice or referral would be helpful before asking someone for assistance.

► **Identify Who Could Help.** Think through your contacts and identify who might be able to provide the information or advice you need. Include people who might be able to connect you with someone else who can help you.

What I Need

_____

_____

_____

_____

Who Might Help

_____

_____

_____

_____

► **Get The Word Out.** Tell people what you are looking for. Don't be shy. Let people know what you need: "I'm looking for a _____ , in case any of you know of one" or "If you come across any _____ , let me know."

► **Express Appreciation.** When someone gives you needed information or a valuable contact, thank him or her. People like to be appreciated. Show appreciation even when the contact may not have worked out.

Appreciation Is Always Welcome

*People Who Have
Helped Me Recently*

_____

_____

_____

*How I Can Show
Appreciation*

_____

_____

_____

SELF-CONTRACT FOR BUILDING SOCIAL SUPPORT

Start building your social support system today. Don't put it off. Review the list of possible things you can do and decide upon one specific action to build your relationship with a friend, family member, co-worker or colleague in your professional organization. Then make a commitment with yourself to take action, *now!*

Use the self-contract. Write down exactly what you are going to do and when you will do it. And remember to give yourself a "win" for following through. You deserve all the "wins" you can get. Make sure to acknowledge your successes.

SELF-CONTRACT FOR
BUILDING SOCIAL RELATIONSHIPS

By (*date*) _____

I will (*small step*) _____

_____

_____

When I complete this I will (*reward from Want List*) _____

_____

_____

Date _____ Signature _____

Summary of Building Social Support

Social support acts as a buffer against the effects of stress. Allies on the job can help you get your job done. Consequently, when you have a strong social support system you feel potent, able to perform well and able to handle the inevitable problems. This helps prevent job burnout.

SKILL BUILDING: THE FOURTH PATH TO PERSONAL POWER

You can't predict what skills the future will demand. Job security depends upon knowing how to acquire needed skills.

Each job skill or ability enlarges your horizons and personal power. You can do more and have more of what you want. Mastery, knowing how *to do* and doing it well, feels good. You like yourself more and get more recognition from others. With self-confidence, you approach difficult situations with an *I-can-do* attitude. It is a chance to exercise your "skill muscles."

By contrast, when you lack needed skills others may claim you represent the Peter Principle because you appear to have reached your "level of incompetence." Without skills necessary to perform, it is difficult to win. Energy is devoted to avoiding negative situations rather than pursuing positive ones. Eventually you feel incompetent, incapable and helpless to change it.

The next few pages will provide some ideas and techniques that will help you build new skills as you need them. The sense of confidence you will derive from acquiring new skills will help you beat job burnout.

See Yourself Learning New Skills

Skill-Building Checklist

Review your Personal Stress Log and your Stress Patterns Analysis. For each situation and pattern, consider what actions you might have taken or what abilities you might have exercised to reduce the distress. Think of others who would have handled the situation more effectively—what skill he or she would have used. For each situation and/or pattern, check the skill identified.

Skill	**Skill**
☐ Assertiveness	☐ Leading meetings
☐ Decision making	☐ Managing time
☐ Listening	☐ Goal setting
☐ Information gathering	☐ Relaxing
☐ Team playing	☐ Self-starting
☐ Delegating	☐ Self-acknowledging
☐ Giving support	☐ Writing
☐ Getting support	☐ Planning
☐ Public speaking	☐ Mediating
☐ Specific technical skills	☐ Giving feedback
☐ Negotiating	☐ Prioritizing
☐ Supervising	☐ Using on-line services
☐ Using feedback	☐ Other
☐ Computing	☐ Other
☐ Mentoring	☐ Other
☐ Networking	☐ Other

Analysis of Skill-Building Checklist

Tally the number of checks for each skill. Circle the five skills with the most checks. These are the skills you need to learn.

SKILL-BUILDING STRATEGIES

Following are several strategies that will help you to build your skills. Check those you plan to begin using.

☐ **ASK FOR FEEDBACK AND ADVICE**

Co-workers and friends see you in ways you don't see yourself. They see you in a more detached way. Ask others what they think you might do to improve your effectiveness at work. Listen to what they say and take advantage of their experience and advice.

☐ **FIND ROLE MODELS**

One of the most effective ways to learn is by watching and copying others. Identify people who are skilled at what you wish to learn. If you can't find anyone on your job or in your personal life, join a club or association, take a course to find role models, or study characters in books or films.

☐ **COACH YOURSELF**

The best teachers are coaches. Coaches use good management techniques. Coaches set reachable targets and praise progress. Coaches give feedback on areas needing improvement and set small-step objectives for the next shot at the target. Coaches are encouraging and supportive. Be your own coach.

☐ **TALK YOURSELF THROUGH**

One of the difficulties in learning a complex skill is that we must do so many different things at the same time. Talking yourself through helps with coordination and keeps you on track.

☐ **FIND A PRACTICE LAB**

Practice is essential in skill building. Identify situations in which you can practice, then actively place yourself in situations that will demand that you use the skill. Set yourself up to win. Begin with easy situations. Sometimes this can be done as a hobby or activity away from the workplace.

☐ **ASSOCIATE WITH PEOPLE WHO HAVE THE SKILL**

Without realizing it, we tend to act like people we spend time with. We pick up their mannerisms, styles or speech, accents and even values. Use this tendency to change yourself. Identify people who are the way that you would like to be and arrange to be around them. This might include social clubs, professional associations, sports groups, work teams—even hangouts.

IDENTIFYING THE SKILL

Clearly define the skill you want to teach yourself and set a goal for the skill level you want to achieve. Set a deadline. Remember to be positive in stating what you wish to learn, to describe the skill on the "doing level" and to create a compelling image of yourself having the skill.

Determine a Small Step. Working backward from the goal, determine the small steps to your achieving the goals and having the skill. Make sure that the steps are small ones. Set yourself up to succeed by selecting the easiest step to begin with.

Set an Objective. Set an objective for achieving the first small step. Remember to make the step small so that it will be easy for you to break your inertia. Require only what you can do easily with a small stretch.

Give Yourself Wins. Create a Want List of things you want and activities you enjoy. Give yourself a reward from your Want List for succeeding in achieving your objective. Make sure to acknowledge your success with positive statements about your performance.

Shape Skills. Like a sculptor creating a statue, accept rough approximations as successes at first. Then using a series of objectives, increase the quality, intensity, degree or length of time of the performance. Reward yourself with items from your Want List and positive thoughts about your successes.

My Skill-Building Plan

Here's another opportunity to use self-management. First, go back and review the Skill Building Checklist. Then fill out your skill-building plan below.

1. *The skill I want to learn or improve is* _____

_____

2. *My skill building goal is (remember to be positive, be specific, create a compelling image and set a deadline)* _____

_____

3. *The small steps I will take are* _____

_____

SELF-CONTRACT FOR
TAKING THE FIRST SKILL-BUILDING STEP

By (*date*) _____

I will (*small step*) _____

_____

_____

When I accomplish this, I will (*reward from Want List*) _____

_____

_____

Date _____ Signature _____

Summary of Skill Building

The modern workplace is constantly changing. We cannot predict the future or know what skills we will need. We must become life-long learners. If you know how to identify the skills you need and arrange a situation for learning them, you will feel confident facing an unknown future. People who can't do this will often find themselves "faking it." Eventually, their performance will decline and their opportunities will evaporate. They will be ripe for job burnout.

TAILORING THE JOB: THE FIFTH PATH TO PERSONAL POWER

A Job That Does Not Fit Will Decrease Your Motivation

Virtually every job has some leeway to tailor it to the person doing the work. Often routines of the job are shaped more by the last person doing it than by the actual task. People forget that jobs are shapeable. Instead, they implement the job in the same style as the last person. When that style doesn't fit, it is like trying to squeeze a round peg into a square hole. Tailor the job to fit you instead. In the process you will increase your personal power because you will feel in command of your work and you will probably do a better job.

Think of this: *You were not hired to do a job, but to solve a problem!* For example, a person is not hired to file papers, but to solve a paper organization problem. What is the major problem you were hired to solve in your current job?

Your purpose is to solve the problem you were hired to solve. One way to identify the problem is to imagine what would happen if no one were dealing with it. That is, try to picture what would happen if the problem went unsolved (sometimes it helps to exaggerate).

> ***My Purpose:*** *It is my responsibility to solve the problem of*

_____

_____

_____

_____

_____

_____

When you know the problem you were hired to solve, then you know what you are to accomplish. Activities that have a big impact on solving the problem are more important and should have a higher priority than those that have less impact.

Rating Tasks and Setting Priorities

First read all the instructions and then complete the following worksheet.

Identify Tasks and Activities: List your tasks and activities at work. If you have difficulty remembering them, close your eyes and see yourself in your work space, doing what you do at work. Notice the various tasks and activities. Do you answer the phone? Complete forms? Meet with co-workers? List as many as you can on the form.

Rate the Impact: Using a scale from 1 to 10, with 1 being "no impact" and 10 being "high impact," rate the effect that each activity has upon the solution you require.

Assign Impact: Use the impact ratings to assign priorities to each task or activity. Assign an "A" priority for tasks with ratings over 7; "B" priority for ratings from 4 to 6; and "C" priority for ratings below 3.

Rate Your Enjoyment: Review the tasks and activities you listed and rate how much you enjoy each, using a scale from 1 to 9, with 1 being "very unpleasant," 5 being "neutral," and 9 being "very pleasurable." Write your enjoyment rating in the last column of the table.

TASK/ACTIVITY	*Impact*	*Priority*	*Enjoyment*
_____	_____	_____	_____
_____	_____	_____	_____
_____	_____	_____	_____
_____	_____	_____	_____
_____	_____	_____	_____
_____	_____	_____	_____
_____	_____	_____	_____
_____	_____	_____	_____
_____	_____	_____	_____
_____	_____	_____	_____

SCHEDULING

You have considerable discretion when you do each task and how much time you spend on it. Are you taking advantage of the flexibility you have or are you doing the job in the same way the last person did it? You can get a lot more done, avoid procrastination, and gain more satisfaction if you manage your tasks instead of letting them manage you.

Use your rating system to schedule your day, start with "A" tasks and activities. Try scheduling them directly in your calendar. Leave "C" priorities until last and—whenever possible—delegate them. What would happen if you did not do the "C" activities at all? If the consequences are minimal, you might consider dropping the activity from your workload.

Managing Your Tasks

TASK MANAGEMENT

You can use tasks you enjoy and tasks you tend to do right away to motivate yourself to do tasks you don't like so much and tend to put off. To do this you must first identify tasks you enjoy and tend to do right away.

Go back to the previous worksheet where you rated tasks and write all of the "A" priority tasks you enjoy doing (those you rated 5 or above in enjoyment) in the column below called "What I Like Doing More." Next, put all the "A" priority tasks you rated 4 or less on enjoyment in the column below called "What I Like Doing Less." Repeat this process with "B" priority and then "C" priority tasks.

Identify Your Tasks

Break complex tasks into several small steps, then list them in the appropriate column.

What I Enjoy	**What I Don't Like**
_____	_____
_____	_____
_____	_____
_____	_____
_____	_____

Now fill out the following with what you currently do on the job and compare it to the items listed above. Are you neglecting any tasks that should be done sooner?

What I Put Off	**What I Do Right Away**
_____	_____
_____	_____
_____	_____
_____	_____

EXPAND YOUR JOB

Jobs are elastic—they can be stretched. Jobs are alive—they can grow and evolve. You can make your job stretch and grow to fit you better.

Here is a strategy for doing that. The best way to expand your job is to identify "unattached problems." These are problems that have not been assigned to any specific person, which means they are available for the taking. Take possession of unattached problems you feel you can solve and that interest you. In most cases, this strategy doesn't require asking permission. You can often just *do* the task and then present it to your supervisor—perhaps obtaining authority after the fact. Depending upon how important the solution is to the company, you might be able to obtain an upgraded job title, add support staff or services, or possibly even get a raise.

Identify Unattached Problems

Close your eyes and *see* yourself at work. Run a typical day across your mental stage. Recall an unusual day, and run it through. Notice what you do and what others do. What problems can you identify? Which fall outside of anyone's responsibility? List them below. While on the job, keep alert for problems, both big and small, that arise and list them. Don't overlook obvious or everyday problems.

For each problem listed ask, "Can I solve it?" Write "S" next to those that you can solve. Next ask, "Does it interest me?" Write "I" next to those that interest you. Problems that receive both an "S" and an "I" are "SI" or "yes" problems. Each of these problems is a potential area for job expansion.

Unattached Problem	I Can Solve It	It Interests Me
_____	_____	_____
_____	_____	_____
_____	_____	_____
_____	_____	_____
_____	_____	_____
_____	_____	_____
_____	_____	_____

Brainstorm Solutions
for Unattached Problems

Review your list of "SI" problems and select one that falls close to your existing responsibilities. Review in your mind the unattached problem you have decided to solve. Just "see" it occurring and study it. Describe the problem:

_____

_____

_____

Now, with your eyes closed, imagine the problem situation "fixed." At this point don't worry about the feasibility of the solution. Just "see" the problem corrected. Describe the solution:

_____

_____

_____

Close your eyes again and see the problem fixed in a different way. Describe the second solution:

_____

_____

_____

Close your eyes again and see the solution fixed in yet a third way. Describe the third solution:

_____

_____

_____

Continue this brainstorming until you come up with a solution that you believe is feasible and that you can implement.

Make a Plan and Take Action

In this exercise you will set a goal for solving an "SI" problem.

My Goal is to (Remember to be positive, be specific, create a compelling image and set a deadline): _____

_____

_____

Now identify the small steps for implementing your solution: _____

_____

_____

_____

Identify Allies

Whose help will you need to implement your solution? List these people: _____

_____

_____

Identify Adversaries

Who might stand in the way or work against your plan? List these people: _____

_____

_____

Identify Resources

What resources will you need to implement your solution? Which allies can help you obtain these resources? List them:

Resource	Ally
_____	_____
_____	_____
_____	_____
_____	_____
_____	_____

FILL OUT THE SELF-CONTRACT
ON THE FOLLOWING PAGE

SELF-CONTRACT: DETERMINE FIRST ACTION OBJECTIVE FOR TAILORING YOUR JOB

By (*date*) _____

I will (*small step*) _____

_____

_____

_____

When I accomplish this I will (*reward from Want List*) _____

_____

_____

_____

Date _____ Signature _____

Summary of Tailoring the Job

If your job doesn't fit your work style you will feel frustrated—and perform less well than you are capable of doing. Over time, such an ill-fitting job can erode your motivation. On the other hand, if you tailor your job to your style of working, you will feel a greater sense of control over your work and reduce the possibility of burning out.

CHANGING JOBS: THE SIXTH PATH TO PERSONAL POWER

Sometimes Changing Jobs Is the Best Way to Prevent Job Burnout.

Some people wait until their job is intolerable, then race blindly into a new job. Without careful analysis and planning, there is little guarantee that the new job will be better. Many times it is worse! Take time to analyze what is bothersome about your job and to determine what would be an ideal job *before* acting. This way you are much more likely to get a job that is right for you. In other words, analyzing what you do and don't like increases your personal power and helps prevent job burnout.

The first question to ask is, "Is the problem with the *type of work* or the *job situation?*" Your answer will help determine if you should change your job or your career.

Consider These Cases

Read the following scenarios and evaluate what each person should do. Compare your responses with those of the author, which are after these cases.

 CASE 1   A nurse enjoys helping patients to understand their medical treatment and to feel more confident about it. But she is constantly at odds with her supervisor who says she's too slow on her rounds.

My recommendation: _____

CASE 2   A nurse enjoys the patients with whom he can chat. But his ward is housing stroke victims, many of whom have difficulty speaking. While intellectually he feels compassionate, he often gets irritated with the patients' slowness. He has snapped at patients more than once. His supervisor has criticized his attitude.

My recommendation: _____

CHANGING JOBS: THE SIXTH PATH TO PERSONAL POWER (continued)

CASE 3   A nurse feels depressed because the patients are annoying her with their constant demands. What little enjoyment there is comes when dealing with record keeping and administrative matters.

My recommendation: _____

Author's Comments

The nurse in Case 1 enjoys her work but is having trouble with her supervisor's style. Changing jobs without first trying to change her job situation would be a mistake. She might solve the problem by learning how to manage her boss.

The nurse in Case 2 enjoys nursing but not the patients assigned to him. Chances are he can learn to control his irritation, but it is unlikely that he will ever like working with nonverbal patients. He is a candidate for job change.

The nurse in Case 3 does not enjoy nursing. She sees patients' problems as demands. She seems to enjoy working with paper more than people. She is a candidate for career change.

Identify Bothersome Situations

Review your Job Burnout Potential Inventory from the first chapter of this book. List each item you rated as 6 or higher on the table below under "Bothersome Situations." Next, close your eyes and project yourself mentally into your typical work day. Review it in your mind and notice what situations tend to make you feel frustrated or helpless. List these bothersome situations. Now bring to mind a particularly distressing day and identify what about it that was bothersome. List these situations. The more specific you are, the better.

Analyze Patterns

Categorize the bothersome aspects of each situation. Use the following categories:

Environment   Noise, poor lighting, crowded, fast pace

Management   Few rewards, little direction, favoritism

Co-workers   Conflicts, politics, cliques, rejection

Type of Work   Writing, servicing, data processing

Other (specify) _____

Now begin the exercise:

Bothersome Situation	**Category**

MY IDEAL JOB

Review your analysis of the bothersome job situations. Which categories predominate? Look closer at those items. What do they have in common? Close your eyes and review each situation in your imagination. What pattern do you see? List the pattern below.

Create a Picture of Your Ideal Job

Make yourself comfortable and use the relaxation technique covered earlier. Let your tension go. With your eyes closed, project one of the patterns listed into your imagination. Observe the bothersome aspect. Jot it down under "Bothersome Situation." Now envision a work situation in which this pattern does not occur. What happens instead? What specific ways is the job different? Note this under "Ideal Scenario." Repeat the exercise several times with each bothersome pattern.

Bothersome Situation:_____

*Ideal Scenario:*_____

Bothersome Situation:_____

*Ideal Scenario:*_____

Bothersome Situation:_____

*Ideal Scenario:*_____

What Is Your Ideal Job?

Envisioning the Ideal Job

Review the factors that you have identified as ideal in a job. Relax and project yourself into this ideal job. Weave in as many aspects of the ideal scenario as possible. What mundane activities would there be? What is the supervision style of your boss? Do you have a boss? What is the environment like? See yourself in the work space. What are co-workers like? Do you socialize with them? Where? Doing what? The more complete the picture of your ideal job, the better. Describe it below. Picture yourself in your ideal job again. Notice what you missed, then add these details to your vision.

My ideal job title is _____

_____

The environment is _____

_____

Management is _____

_____

My boss is _____

_____

Co-workers are _____

_____

The mundane parts of the job are _____

_____

The interesting parts of the job are _____

_____

Other aspects of the job are _____

_____

Transforming Barriers into Challenges

Under "Barriers," list everything standing between where you are now and your ideal job. Under "Challenges," list what you must do to remove the barrier. Don't be "realistic." Just write down what it would take to get around the barrier. Notice what you are thinking when you do this exercise. If you hear yourself saying a lot of reasons why you can't, then list "negative thinking" as one of the barriers. Overcoming negative thinking is one of the greatest challenges of all.

Barriers	**Challenges**
_____	_____
_____	_____
_____	_____
_____	_____
_____	_____

His Barriers Are Removed!

MAKE A PLAN AND ACT

You can move toward your ideal job! Use the self-management techniques discussed earlier for a winning approach. Choose a challenge, make a plan of action and then work on it in small steps. Make sure that you give yourself "wins" for success. Each day you will be a little closer to your ideal job. Each day you will feel more in control of your work and your life. Each day you will be taking action to prevent job burnout.

Choose a Challenge

Review your list of Barriers and Challenges and select a challenge to work on.

To meet my challenge I will have to _____

_____

My goal is _____

_____

_____

_____

_____

Small steps to take are _____

_____

_____

_____

_____

SELF-CONTRACT FOR GETTING STARTED IN CHANGING JOBS

By (*date*) _____

I will (*small step*) _____

_____

_____

When I accomplish this I will (*reward from Want List*) _____

_____

_____

Date _____ Signature _____

Summary of Changing Jobs

Sometimes the best way to prevent job burnout is to get a new job. Don't act impulsively, however. It is very important to pinpoint exactly what about the job is dampening your motivation—as well as what would refuel it. This information will help you to feel more confident in your job search, to increase the chances that you will get a job that fits you and to prevent burning out.

THINKING POWERFULLY: THE SEVENTH PATH TO PERSONAL POWER

*Powerful Thinking Is Looking at the Glass
Half Full Rather Than as Half Empty*

Your mind is always filled with thoughts and images. The mental chatter is always there. And the thoughts and images in your mind determine your mood.

If you think powerless thoughts and envision yourself as losing, you will feel powerless: depressed, anxious, frustrated, angry. These feelings bring on job burnout.

Do you carry your frustrations with you?

The Muddy Road: A Zen Story

Two monks were walking along a muddy road when they came upon a beautiful woman unable to cross the road without getting her silk shoes muddy. Without saying a word, the first monk picked her up and carried the woman across the road, leaving her on the other side. Then the two monks continued walking without talking until the end of the day. When they reached their destination, the second monk said, "You know monks should avoid women. Why did you pick up that woman this morning?" The first monk replied, "I left her on the side of the road. Are you still carrying her?"

If you think powerful thoughts and envision yourself as winning, you will feel powerful: hopeful, enthusiastic, confident, energized. These feelings help prevent job burnout.

Leave Your Problems on
the Side of the Road.

Get In Touch with Your Mood

Notice how you feel. Survey your body and emotions. Using a scale from 1 to 10, with 1 being "very negative," and 10 being "very positive," rate how you feel right now.

My mood rating _____

Make your mind blank—a blank mind contains no thoughts, no images, no colors. Nothing at all. Keep your mind blank for 60 seconds.

What happened? Did thoughts intrude and images scurry by? It is impossible for most people to make their minds blank without intensive mental training. Your mind is constantly filled with thoughts and images.

Recall an *unpleasant situation.* For 60 seconds, project yourself back into that scene. Make it as vivid as possible. Notice how your body feels and how you respond. Rate your mood again, using the same 1 to 10 scale.

My mood rating: _____

Physical sensations I experienced: _____

_____

What I experienced during the actual situation: _____

_____

You Feel What You Think

Now recall a *pleasant situation*. For 60 seconds, relive a time when you were feeling good and doing well, making it as vivid as possible. Notice how your body feels and how you respond. Rate your mood again, using the same 1 to 10 scale.

My mood rating: _____

Physical sensations I experienced: _____

_____

What I experienced during the actual situation: _____

_____

What happened? Did your mood state drop after recalling the unpleasant situation? What happened to your body? Did you feel tension? Did your heart race? How did your body react in the actual situation? Was it similar? How did you feel after recalling the pleasant time?

NEGATIVE THOUGHTS WITH AN I-CAN-DO ATTITUDE!

DEVELOP AN *I-CAN-DO* ATTITUDE

Attitude is a style of thinking. People with *no-can-do* attitudes think negatively and feel powerless. They continually tell themselves that they "can't." People who think positively focus on what they *can* do. They have an *I-can-do* attitude. Consequently, they feel powerful. They feel optimistic. They rise to challenges. No-can-do thinking makes you feel bad. It can even damage your health. I-can-do thinking fuels motivation and helps prevent job burnout.

Rid yourself of negative thinking. Translate each powerless thought into a powerful one. Powerful thoughts make you feel potent and help you act to influence the situation for the better.

Powerless Thought	Powerful Thought
− How could I have been so stupid?	+ I made a mistake and I can learn from my mistakes.
− I really blew it this time. I'm a fool!	+ Next time I can . . .
− My boss is such a lousy supervisor. I never know what he expects.	+ It would be nice if my boss would be clear in his expectations. This is my chance to practice my assertive skills. I must learn how to express my concern without alienating him.
− I might lose control and start yelling at them. I'd better take a tranquilizer.	+ I'll make a plan for what I can do to handle my temper. Next time I can . . .
− She is so inconsiderate of me.	+ I'd like it if she'd call when she's late but she doesn't. Figuring out how to handle this is a challenge. Next time I can . . .

Change Your Thoughts to Powerful Ones

Listen to your thinking. When you think a powerless thought list it below. Include all the reasons you tell yourself for not doing what you want to do—faults, failures and disappointments that you think about. Include others' wrongdoings that haunt you, guilts you worry about, other negative thoughts you ruminate about. After you've collected several powerless thoughts, translate each powerless thought into a more powerful way of describing the situation.

Powerless Thought	**Powerful Thought**
_____	_____
_____	_____
_____	_____
_____	_____
_____	_____

Thinking Powerfully Feels Better!

THOUGHT STOPPING: CONTROLLING NEGATIVE THOUGHTS

The Mind Is Like a Wild Elephant

The mind is like a wild elephant that you must master. In mastering a wild elephant you begin by chaining it. But when first chained, it rears up on its hind legs, throws its trunk back and roars. It flaps its ears, slaps its tail and runs. If you are a good elephant trainer you don't scold the elephant, but simply grab the chain and pull it back. The elephant will try to run away again. When this happens you must pull it back again. Again and again the elephant will rebel—and again and again you must pull it back. Eventually, the elephant will be tamed when it learns that you are its master. Then you will have great power because you can climb up on the elephant and ride it. And the elephant no longer will have to wear its chain because it learned who its master is.

Mastering Your Wild Mind

▶ **Think the Powerless Thought.** Close your eyes and begin thinking one of your powerless thoughts. Repeat it over and over in your mind in the way that you typically do. Notice how you feel as you do this.

▶ **Then Yell "Stop!"** Inside your mind, not out loud (unless you are alone), yell "Stop!" at the powerless thought.

▶ **Switch to the Powerful Thought.** Immediately change to a powerful thought. If the powerless thought creeps back in, just yell "Stop!" again, and pull your attention back to the powerful thought. No matter how many times your mind runs to the powerless thought, pull it back to the powerful one, again and again. Notice how you feel while thinking the powerful thought. Repeat this practice several times with each of the powerless thoughts.

▶ **Watch Your Thoughts.** Whenever you catch yourself thinking one of your powerless thoughts, yell "Stop!" and pull your mind back to the powerful one. Acknowledge yourself for your successes in mastering your mind.

▶ **Practicing.** We never have our minds fully trained. Rather, we can get better and better with practice. At least once a day, tell yourself to think one of your powerful thoughts. Develop a habit of talking powerfully to yourself. Compliment yourself whenever you notice yourself thinking a powerful thought.

```
❧

# SELF-CONTRACT FOR
# THINKING MORE POWERFULLY


**For** (how long) _____

**I will** (small step or technique) _____

_____

_____


**I will acknowlede my progress by** (reward from want list) _____

_____

_____


Date _____    Signature _____

❧
```

Summary of Thinking Powerfully

Your mood is determined by the thoughts in your mind. Chronic powerless thinking is a major contributor to job burnout. When you think powerfully you feel more powerful—and are better equipped to take action to correct distressing situations at work and at home.

DETACHED CONCERN: THE EIGHTH PATH TO PERSONAL POWER

*Detached Concern Is a Delicate Balance
of Involvement and Nonattachment*

Helping professionals must demonstrate concern for clients to be effective. But there is a danger of overinvolvement. What if the client doesn't improve? Salespeople are expected to sell. What if the economy is in a recession? Teachers want to teach. What if the students won't learn? What if you have a truly impossible job? What if the "wins" are too few and there is nothing you can do? What if your job is terrible but you can't change it and can't leave it? Here are a few guidelines to follow.

Good Sportsmanship

Play to win (be concerned), but don't insist upon winning (be detached). Athletes who *must win* inevitably fumble and lose. How you shoot the arrow is more important than hitting the target. Whatever job you hold, immerse yourself in the moment, in the *doing*, and let go of the outcome, good or bad. Don't demand wins. Events will not always be to your liking and you will not always win. Let losing teach you how to shoot the arrow next time. But don't cling to losing, either. Like the monk walking along the muddy road, leave the negative situation on the side of the road.

Sportsmanship

The Mirror Principle

The mirror teaches "acceptance" or nonevaluation. When you step before a mirror, it reflects you. It doesn't evaluate who you are or wonder if it should reflect you. It simply reflects. The mirror exhibits "concern" because it reflects you totally and not half-heartedly. It does the best it can. And the mirror teaches "detachment." When you step away from the mirror it stops reflecting you. It doesn't protest; it simply lets you go.

Mother Teresa

A reporter asked, "You work with sick and dying children and they die anyway. How can you stand it?" The Nobel Prize-winning nun replied, "We love them while they are here." Mother Teresa is concerned and loves the children, yet she is detached. If they die, she lets them go.

Be Here Now

A monk was walking through the jungle when he encountered a hungry tiger. So he ran until he came to a ravine with a vine hanging over the edge. He climbed down until he saw a hungry tiger below. Safe for the moment, he listened and heard the gnawing noise of mice chewing on the vine. The monk was doomed. So he looked about and saw a strawberry plant with one luscious berry growing from the side of the ravine. He popped it into his mouth, and just as the vine snapped, he said, "Ah, delicious!" Don't dwell on past problems or worries about the future. Live fully in the present moment—whatever you are doing.

Be Yielding

Be flexible. Like water flowing downstream, flow around the rocks in life. Don't be attached to a particular notion of the way things ought to be. Look for alternative and creative ways to reach your goals.

Shift Your Viewpoint

Philosopher Alan Watts once said, "Problems that remain persistently insolvable should always be suspected as questions asked in the wrong way." Do you trap yourself in damned-if-you-do, damned-if-you-don't situations by the way you look at things? Think about things in new ways. See problems as opportunities, and hassles as teachers.

DETACHED CONCERN: THE EIGHTH PATH TO PERSONAL POWER (continued)

Laugh a Lot

When you catch yourself taking things too seriously, laugh. Think of the "cosmic chuckle" and of the absurdity of it all. Satirize your distress. Imagine yourself in a Charley Chaplin script. As a discipline, practice finding humor in disaster. You'll save your sanity, your health and your perspective.

SELF-CONTRACT FOR PRACTICING DETACHED CONCERN

For *(how long)* _____

I will *(small step or technique)* _____

_____

_____

I will acknowlede my progress by *(reward from want list)* _____

_____

_____

Date _____   Signature _____

Summary of Detached Concern

If your job is distressing and you cannot change it or leave it, then strive for detached concern. Make your best effort and don't dwell upon whether you are winning or losing. Instead, roll with the punches, focus on the present, think of problems as opportunities and make sure to laugh a lot.

SUMMARY

1. Job burnout is an impairment of enthusiasm and motivation caused by feelings of powerlessness at work. It is a destructive process that affects the victim's health, relationships and performance. Common burnout symptoms include frequent illness, feelings of fatigue, irritability, substance abuse, withdrawal, absenteeism and declining job performance.

2. Burnout can be prevented by adequate amounts of motivational nutrients. "Wins" are essential to maintaining high levels of motivation. Wins include acknowledgment, feelings of satisfaction, rewards and other positive outcomes for doing good work.

   You must also have at least some *feeling of control.* To remain motivated you must feel that you can influence what happens to you by what you do.

3. Burnout is cured by developing *personal power.* Personal power is a feeling of "I can do," a feeling that you can act to increase the wins and reduce the losses you receive. Personal power is a feeling of potency, a feeling that you can influence others and change situations in desired ways.

4. There are many paths to personal power. The eight covered in this book are as follows:

   Self-Management is using techniques such as goal setting and self-acknowledgment to sustain motivation and do what you set out to do.

   Stress Management is identifying stress factors and moderating your physical and emotional responses to them for maximum health and performance.

   Building Social Support increases your effectiveness on the job and buffers you from the effects of stress.

   Skill Building helps you adapt to a changing workplace, increases your effectiveness and promotes self-confidence.

   Tailoring the Job to you makes working more enjoyable and maximizes your ability to perform at your peak.

SUMMARY (continued)

Changing Jobs removes you from the burnout situation. However, finding the right job for you requires analysis of the burnout factors in your old job and insight into your work style and interests.

Powerful Thinking leads to an I-can-do attitude. The way you think influences how you feel. Negative thinking underlies anger and depression, but powerful thinking promotes feelings of personal power.

Detached Concern helps you to deal with situations that you cannot change and that offer few wins.

5. Developing personal power is not a one-time endeavor. Rather, it is a lifelong process of learning how to handle difficult situations.

NOTES

NOTES

NOTES

NOTES

NOTES

NOW AVAILABLE FROM CRISP PUBLICATIONS

Books • Videos • CD Roms • Computer-Based Training Products

If you enjoyed this book, we have great news for you. There are over 200 books available in the *50-Minute*™ Series. To request a free full-line catalog, contact your local distributor or Crisp Publications, Inc., 1200 Hamilton Court, Menlo Park, CA 94025. Our toll-free number is 800-442-7477.

Subject Areas Include:

Management

Human Resources

Communication Skills

Personal Development

Marketing/Sales

Organizational Development

Customer Service/Quality

Computer Skills

Small Business and Entrepreneurship

Adult Literacy and Learning

Life Planning and Retirement

CRISP WORLDWIDE DISTRIBUTION

English language books are distributed worldwide. Major international distributors include:

ASIA/PACIFIC

Australia/New Zealand: In Learning, PO Box 1051, Springwood QLD, Brisbane, Australia 4127   Tel: 61-7-3-841-2286, Facsimile: 61-7-3-841-1580
ATTN: Messrs. Gordon

Singapore: 85, Genting Lane, Guan Hua Warehouse Bldng #05-01, Singapore 349569   Tel: 65-749-3389, Facsimile: 65-749-1129
ATTN: Evelyn Lee

Japan: Phoenix Associates Co., LTD., Mizuho Bldng. 3-F, 2-12-2, Kami Osaki, Shinagawa-Ku, Tokyo 141   Tel: 81-33-443-7231, Facsimile: 81-33-443-7640
ATTN: Mr. Peter Owans

CANADA

Reid Publishing, Ltd., Box 69559-109 Thomas Street, Oakville, Ontario Canada L6J 7R4.   Tel: (905) 842-4428, Facsimile: (905) 842-9327
ATTN: Mr. Stanley Reid

Trade Book Stores: *Raincoast Books*, 8680 Cambie Street, Vancouver, B.C., V6P 6M9   Tel: (604) 323-7100, Facsimile: (604) 323-2600
ATTN: Order Desk

EUROPEAN UNION

England: *Flex Training*, Ltd. 9-15 Hitchin Street, Baldock, Hertfordshire, SG7 6A, England   Tel: 44-1-46-289-6000, Facsimile: 44-1-46-289-2417
ATTN: Mr. David Willetts

INDIA

Multi-Media HRD, Pvt., Ltd., National House, Tulloch Road, Appolo Bunder, Bombay, India 400-039   Tel: 91-22-204-2281, Facsimile: 91-22-283-6478
ATTN: Messrs. Aggarwal

SOUTH AMERICA

Mexico: *Grupo Editorial Iberoamerica*, Nebraska 199, Col. Napoles, 03810 Mexico, D.F.   Tel: 525-523-0994, Facsimile: 525-543-1173
ATTN: Señor Nicholas Grepe

SOUTH AFRICA

Alternative Books, Unit A3 Micro Industrial Park, Hammer Avenue, Stridom Park, Randburg, 2194 South Africa   Tel: 27-11-792-7730, Facsimile: 27-11-792-7787
ATTN: Mr. Vernon de Haas